BITCH FIGHT

VANESSA VERSHAW

JEAN-FRANÇOIS DUCHARME

An Artistic Warrior Publication

AW

Artistic Warrior

Ordering Information:

Quantity sales. Special discounts are available on quantity purchases by corporations, libraries, associations, and others. For details, contact the authors at: orders@bitchfight.com.au

Visit our website at bitchfight.com.au

Team Published with Artistic Warrior.

Library and Archives Canada Cataloguing in Publication

Ducharme, Jean-François, author

Bitch fight: put an end to women bullying women in the workplace / Jean-François Ducharme, Vanessa Vershaw.

Issued also in electronic format.

ISBN 978-1-987982-07-7 (paperback).

--ISBN 978-1-987982-08-4

1. Bullying in the workplace. 2. Women employees--Psychology. I. Vershaw, Vanessa, author II. Title.

HF5549.5.E43D82 2016   658.3'8

C2015-908267-6

C2015-908268-4

This book was inspired by true events.

DISCLAIMER

While this story is inspired by true events, all names and company names have been changed to protect the guilty and the innocent.

This book is dedicated to our daughters Allegra Lia and Marilou Catherine. May it provide you with the conviction to stand up for your beliefs, the courage to be trailblazers, the wisdom to get ahead and the freedom to shine brightly.

Contents

Part One

Chapter 1	The Opportunity	5
Chapter 2	The Contenders	7
Chapter 3	Ready, Aim, Fire!	10
Chapter 4	Balls the Size of Grapefruits	12
Chapter 5	Backfire	14
Chapter 6	Keeping it Real	17
Chapter 7	Tapped Out	19
Chapter 8	Talk is Cheap	20
Chapter 9	Leather Whips and Chains	22
Chapter 10	It's Showtime	25
Chapter 11	Rollercoaster Ride	27
Chapter 12	A Wolf in Sheep's Clothing	29
Chapter 13	Who's Your Daddy	30
Chapter 14	The Disappearance of Kathryn	31
Chapter 15	Dark Shadows	32
Chapter 16	Divine Retribution	34

Part Two

Chapter 17	It's a Man's World	39
Chapter 18	It's All About Sex	46
Chapter 19	Word from the Street	50
Chapter 20	Standing Up to the Female Bully	55
Chapter 21	Enter the Psychopath	59
Chapter 22	No More Miss Nice Girl	64
Chapter 23	Welcome to the Jungle	68
Chapter 24	Are You a Potential Target?	77
Chapter 25	Make Love, Not War	82

About the Authors	85

*There's a special place in hell reserved for women who
don't help other women.*

Madeleine Albright, Former US Secretary of State

Preface

It's January 2008 and I'm in Boston. Temperatures are an Arctic -40 degrees and the snow has turned into icy rain. No matter where I turn I get a frigid slap in the face. By 9 a.m. I had run five kilometres on an indoor treadmill, watched CNN, taken a ride in a Toronto taxi, and had three tasteless cappuccinos at the airport while awaiting my flight. Now I was in Boston in the boardroom on the top floor of a well-known American bank. I was there to meet with the executive team and talk them into spending big bucks. I would show them how to do a better job of harnessing the potential in their organisation and release their next generation of leaders. That's one of the joys of believing you are Wonder Woman. You push yourself so hard that you start to believe you're infallible. You're so controlled and over-prepared that nothing can ever go wrong.

Back to the boardroom. The 180-degree views of the Atlantic Ocean and Boston Harbour are spectacular. I secretly congratulate myself. I know I've got this gig in the bag. As a senior executive of a well-known human capital company, I've been schmoozing this mob for months. Today was the day I was going to seal the deal. I'd already planned my celebration. Since I was going to be spending so much time in Boston, I decided after they'd signed off on the contract I'd treat myself and buy a season's pass to catch Red Sox games at Fenway Park. I was really pumped.

Nothing could have been further from reality. You see, back at my head office, there was an operations manager called Tiffany who had delusions of grandeur. She was secretly plotting my demise. Tiffany had made her way into a professional position by having razor-sharp street smarts and a burning hunger to succeed. It amazed me how in an elitist organisation like ours, where educational pedigree was everything, she had even made it through the door.

Tiffany was charged with preparing the sales materials for the session, which included setting up the video-conferencing technology. We were going to wow our Boston clients with interactive charts, live video streaming and the benefit of Tiffany's insights around on-line talent assessment systems.

I'm juiced and ready. I take my position at the head of the boardroom table, poised and ready for the show. I decided not to show them the usual PowerPoint slides. Instead, I would dazzle them with my showmanship and talk them through the glossy information packs. Being an infotainer is a critical skill to master when you're a human capital consultant. You need to be memorable and I was determined not to leave the meeting empty handed.

As the executive team members open their packs I realized something was very wrong. I was met with a succession of confused looks as their team stared at me. I picked one of the packs up to discover it was empty!

I didn't let it get to me as I am the queen of cool. I'm the one who stays calm under pressure. I know I can handle this. I have had to wing it many times before; this would be no different. I'd use the whiteboard. I can do this. I'm feeling rather smug about my over-preparedness and my impressive skills of improvisation. I will triumph and save the day.

Everyone settles and Tiffany appears on the big screen. I don't let my hostility show. I'll deal with her later. Suddenly we hear a child's scream. Tiffany runs off camera saying something about her son falling and cracking his head open. Then the screen goes blank.

Silence.

I never saw that executive team again.

The next two months went from bad to worse. Losing that opportunity threw my competence into question. Unbeknownst to me, Tiffany had been undermining me for months. She'd taken advantage of my absence as I travelled around the country. She cast doubt on my leadership competence to secure her position as next in line. She had gifted tickets to a Toronto Raptors game to my executive assistant, gotten mighty chummy with the CFO, and fudged my sales pipeline. When the shit hit the fan, it landed all over me.

Tiffany's edge was to present herself as the underdog trying to make a go of it in a world she wanted so desperately to be part of. I provided a stark contrast to Tiffany and fit all the criteria to make it. To her, there was a target on my back that flashed in full Technicolor.

The ending was textbook. I grew weary of dodging the heavy artillery fire that came my way on a daily basis. I felt like I was fighting a battle I couldn't win so I left the company. My faith in my boss and what he stood for had taken a nosedive. I fired the organisation from my life and divorced my boss.

I learned some big life lessons from that time of my life. As for regrets, I do have one. I regret I didn't let Tiffany go when I had the chance. My boss had given me the opportunity after a number of her earlier transgressions like overriding my authority on key business decisions in my absence and hurling foul-mouthed abuse at other team members in public view. At the time I flat out turned him down.

To be honest I know that I had been more concerned about playing the nice-girl card than I was about getting results. I was guilty of what Facebook COO Sheryl Sandberg describes as the curse we women have of trying to be liked at all costs, even at our own expense. My decision to be nice and my fear of the dreaded bitch label led to my departure and saying goodbye to the corner office.

My story is not unusual. As coaches and psychologists for over three decades, Jean-François and I have coached countless male and female leaders who have shared similar tales involving powerful, destructive women, often with worse outcomes.

What is interesting, though, is that whether our clients have been in bitch fights themselves or have witnessed others having the experience, the deleterious psychological impact often runs deep and can last a lifetime.

The good news for me is that my fall from grace was short lived. Yes, the bullying experience left a sting, but it also presented a formidable professional growth opportunity. I realised how much our strong need for approval as women can limit our potential.

Women will often significantly diminish their own sphere of influence by focusing on maintaining relationships at the expense of getting results. So how do we as women stop our natural need for keeping the peace at all costs? We can start by stopping with our nauseating apologising, toss out some of the tact and constructively confront the bullies in our lives.

Elizabeth Gilbert, author of the popular novel Eat, Pray, Love, sums up the essence of our book so well when she said: "The women whom I love and admire for their grace and strength did not get that way because shit worked out. They got that way because shit went wrong and they handled it. They handled it in a thousand different ways, on a thousand different days, but they handled it. Those women are my superheroes."

This book is a celebration of everyday women overcoming extraordinary obstacles to rise stronger than ever before. They are our inspiration for writing this book.

Introduction

Whack! Crack! Thud! Did you hear that sound? It happened again. Another woman just cracked her head on that impenetrable glass ceiling. Her head is bloodied and throbs with a dull ache. It sucks to be her.

But whose fault is it? Contrary to popular belief, it's not men that are always the perpetrators. Women mistreating their sisters in business are at the root of many women's inability to move up the corporate ladder. It's a key contributor to the battle for women to achieve equality in the workplace.

As workplace coaches, we have witnessed just about every heinous workplace crime known to man. Watching successful professional women behave badly towards other women at work remains one of the more disgraceful displays of primitive and corrosive behaviour we have ever seen. The behaviour has reached epic proportions in the modern-day workplace. It's one of the major sources of competitive disadvantages for organisations worldwide.

How is it that even though the incidence of women sabotaging other women at work is pervasive, it still remains a phenomenon cloaked in silence? Perhaps it is because most people don't want to talk about it and/or they don't know what to do about it. They fear being labelled politically incorrect or discriminatory. Quite simply, it's a subject that remains taboo and it isn't given any air-time.

With each closed mouth and awkward silence the issue of women mistreating other women at work remains an invisible threat. It can result in decimated careers, cause organisational decline, and leave broken people in its wake.

We wrote this book for all those whose lives have been turned upside down, in the spirit of providing them hope. We'd like to share our strategies, insights and understanding of the what, the how and the why. We want to help you deal with the bullies at work who may be making your life hell or preventing you from having the job and career that you want and deserve.

About this Book

This is a book about female-on-female bullying in the workplace. Our goal is to describe the phenomenon from all angles, build some coping skills for anyone who has gone or is going through it, and subsequently prevent its future occurrence.

Part One of this book begins with a leadership story because we have found that some of the best learning happens when people can identify and draw meaning from real situations and characters.

"Kathryn's Story" is the tale of a talented and successful executive who takes a stab at the CEO position in her company. This story illustrates the corruption and tactics of multiple players in her organisation who try to stop her getting the job. Inspired by true events, Kathryn's story illustrates what can really happen when a woman makes a play for the top job in a traditionally male-dominated family business.

We will take you through her journey and comment on it from our perspective as coaching professionals, providing several coaching insights. We'll show you how a coach thinks and feels and what is said during a coaching session, illustrating how insights come to light, how pitfalls are overcome, and how change happens. We give you the critical information you need in order to spot workplace psychopaths and avoid their traps.

In Part Two, "Reality Check," we draw on a combined 30 years of experience as psychologists and coaches to provide solutions on how to deal with situations involving women bullies at work. We offer our views and guidance to equip you with the skills to manage these situations and come out on top.

In creating this book, we had to put the phenomenon into context. When you understand what's really going on, it helps you sharpen your skills.

"It's a Man's World" presents the facts as to how far women have progressed and how far away they still are from their destination. To believe that women have truly made great strides forward toward equality is akin to believing in Father Christmas and the Easter Bunny. This chapter provides the straight dope on the current state of play and sets the stage for understanding how much women are held back by organisational systems and traditional beliefs.

In "It's All About Sex," we turn things upside down and take on the quest of understanding the root of women-on-women fighting. This takes us back to the beginning of time and the explanation we found might not be what you expect. We will tackle it from the ground up and discuss how women have the power to better manage their biases toward other women and halt an irresistible urge to some downright mean behaviours.

Next up is a "Word from the Street" where we take a deeper look at all the taboos related to workplace female bullying and find out why so many resist talking about it and acknowledging its devastating impact on so many people. The chapter closes with a lesson in honesty that is well worth meditating over.

Knowledge is power, and in "Portrait of a Female Bully" we explore who the bullies are. At the same time, we debunk some persistent myths about regular folks, bitches, and psychopaths. Key information about the vicious bullying cycle one can get caught up in is brought to the fore. You'll learn what type of fertile soil can favour the of a Queen Bee. We'll show you how to deal with the difficult person so many of us are ill equipped to cope with effectively.

In "Welcome to the Jungle" we look at it from the male perspective. You may be surprised by how unaware men are of women-on-women bullying in the workplace. Learn how responses change when they have a daughter, sister or wife on the receiving end of bullying. Their answers are quite illuminating and help us move forward.

For those who think that you can successfully avoid dealing with the bitches in your workplace, think again. Dodging this issue will leave you worse off, either leaving the organisation or becoming a victim. Bottom line: it is not an intelligent career strategy.

However, learning to better manage bullying behaviours at work will lead to increased overall personal and organisational productivity and effectiveness. It is both achievable and sustainable. We wrap up the book with chapters devoted to helping leaders manage this rampant threat and build competitive advantage for both themselves and the company they work for.

Whichever way you slice it, we hope that our book provides you with some relief and the information you need to tackle your fears and turn any bitch situation into a competitive advantage. We hope that all of you turn the everyday into the extraordinary to become the superheroes of your own lives.

BITCH FIGHT

PART ONE

Kathryn's Story

CHAPTER 1 – THE OPPORTUNITY

This is the story of Kathryn, a forty-year-old woman who decided to put her hat into the ring for CEO of Kudos Industries. Kudos Industries was an organisation specialising in the development of on-line betting systems for sports racing and gaming agencies. Kathryn's title was "General Manager of Marketing and Strategy" and she had been with Kudos for twelve years.

She graduated top of her class in law at a prestigious ivy-league school in the United States. Offers for internship had come in thick and fast, but she turned them all down for a role in the marketing department of a reputable airline whose brand was sexy and world-class and whose leader was famous for his gregarious character, fearless nature, and penchant for taking creative risks. Her decision paid off and several years later she was well known in the industry as a product and marketing seer with the gift of foresight and a nose for the next best thing. Joining Kudos was a big career move. The lure of working in a start-up organisation in the technology sector enticed her. The thought of having an opportunity to create a new market sector was too good to pass up. She had learned a lot from her role with the airline; however, now it was time to test herself without the crutch of her previous boss.

Kudos Industries' headquarters was located Toronto, the industrial hub of Eastern Canada. Like many fast-growing Toronto-based companies, the culture at Kudos was all about stealth, entrepreneurial genius and world domination. Peter Stringer, its founder, was a charismatic, hard-driving powerhouse full of great ideas with incredible skills of execution and the additional incentive of having to prove to everyone that he was just as successful as his father.

Cornelius Stringer had made his millions thirty years earlier buying up forests in small towns in northern Ontario and building pulp and paper processing plants to provide Canadians with enough toilet tissue to wipe their bottoms clean. Investing in a green-fields enterprise and entrusting the building of his fortune to his oldest son meant that he watched the rise of Kudos with obsessive scrutiny. He placed enormous pressure on his son to succeed. There was also the threat of disinheritance if anything should go wrong.

So, with an almighty chip on his shoulder and massive shoes to fill, Peter had created a take-no-prisoners culture at Kudos: to win business at all costs, to value results at the expense of relationships. This ensured a FIFO (fit in or f*ck off) approach to managing performance.

A decision to step back from the CEO role and focus more on innovation and developing other lines of business created an unprecedented opportunity for someone else to take the helm and lead Kudos.

The all-male (except for Kathryn) executive team had been with the organisation since its inception. They had enjoyed the fruits of a business that had a monopoly on the gaming industry; Kudos' on-line solutions provided the software to most betting engines in North America. They were a market force to be reckoned with. The likelihood of Kathryn successfully winning the role was next to nil given the testosterone-high, incestuous culture of the business, but she decided to go for it anyway.

Kathryn called us in the final days of her preparation to help her take her game to the next level. As her coaches and trusted advisors, we got to witness her battle first hand – the good, the bad and the ugly. This is her story.

CHAPTER 2 – THE CONTENDERS

Kathryn Underwood

We first met Kathryn six years earlier. She was 34 at the time and had just said "I do" to Bruce, an old flame she had briefly dated back in high-school. She and Bruce had rekindled their relationship at their high school reunion in their picturesque home town of Wakefield, Quebec, about 35 kilometres from Canada's capital city of Ottawa.

As coaches, we were struck by Kathryn's talent, leadership potential and striking good looks. Kathryn had piercing sea-blue eyes and long, silky auburn tresses she kept tied up in a pony-tail to keep the focus on her professional persona. She attributed her statuesque, trim and taut figure to her mother, clean eating, and a relentless dedication to yoga five times a week.

Despite her attempts to downplay her physical attributes, Kathryn could not hide her beauty. It was fascinating for us to watch people meet her for the first time, men in particular. They'd gawk and fumble, mutter, and splutter in her presence. Even we had to stop ourselves from staring at this woman – she was a goddess. Her external appearance was rivalled by her astute intellect, creative mind, and down-to-earth personality. She was unaware of how magnificent she really was.

Kathryn had the world at her feet, but she kept getting in her own way. She cared too much about what others thought of her. Her need for approval was so high that it made her appear weak and indecisive. She put other people first, at the expense of herself and getting results.

In her personal life, a history of failed relationships echoed her issues around surrendering herself and her own need to be the proverbial door-mat. It was amazing to see how, in the face of finding love, such an extraordinary woman diminished her own light to a dull and wavering flicker.

She wasn't sure when she had made her decision to compete for the top job, and now she had reached the tipping point: there was no turning back. Going public with her decision sealed her fate. She put it all on the line. No more second-guessing herself, no more pussy-footing around.

When we reconnected with Kathryn, being a supporting act had become a thing of the past for her. She had undergone a mammoth personal transformation. Heartbreak will do that to you. Her decision to marry Bruce had been a safe option after being trampled on too many times by foreign playboys who had whispered sweet nothings in Mediterranean tongues. They had promised her the world and never delivered. Bruce was a reliable and stoic bookworm-ish guy who made a good living as a well-known philatelist. (That's the study of stamps and postal history and other related items.)

Methodical and matter-of-fact, he was the antithesis of her previous gushing flames. His word was his bond. Kathryn traded passion for loyalty and excitement for familiarity. Bruce would never break her heart. The relationship had strengthened her. The princess had toughened up.

As a leader she was now more focused on driving results through others and leading from behind. Some may even have described her as cold. From our perspective, Kathryn had become more of a fighter. She was courageous and strong. Her team was committed and loyal to her. Kathryn had proven that she could get results.

It had been a long time coming and Kathryn was ready to rumble – she was willing to put the gloves on and fight for what she wanted, and she wanted it real bad. But did she have what it takes to be the new CEO of Kudos? Would she be recognised by others as having the X factor? Would she be able to come out on top?

Preston Steele

Kathryn's competition for the CEO job was Preston Steele. He had more sizzle than a sausage. One might say his middle name was sleaze. Preston was the kind of guy that slithered around dripping words smothered in honey. He was the kind of guy who could get away with murder. We'd seen him in action from afar, and this man was fierce when he worked a room. Ask just about anyone what they thought about the latest fool he double-crossed or any one of the string of women he left broken hearted, and the response was usually "Oh, that's just Preston."

Preston was not a wimpy yet oh-so-cool metrosexual. He was a ruggedly handsome man with a powerful physique. Well built, in his early forties, Preston's well-styled salt-and-pepper hair gave him the illusion of wisdom beyond his years. His naturally olive skin and doe-brown eyes contrasted against snow-white teeth to present a perfect picture of health. It was difficult not to notice him. He was the ultimate snake charmer. Growing up next to a steel mill in the industrial city of Hamilton, Ontario, had given him the motivation to leave behind his impoverished existence with his single mom. He jumped into a new life and never looked back. His mother was lucky if she heard from him at all. There was the odd Christmas card, but it usually arrived late because he'd forgotten to mail it on time.

His background in a cut-throat sales environment equipped him with the skills to play dirty and win. Preston was the consummate political animal.

He had mastered the art of networking with all the right people. People either opened the doors for him or kept him out of trouble. From all accounts, he was not particularly smart or driven; however, he was as slick as they come. His greatest gift was the ability to sweet talk people into doing things for him. Preston was all about minimum effort for high return and all the glory that went with it. We were impressed that he'd made it this far. He had humble beginnings as a door-to-door vacuum cleaner salesman to a menagerie of bored and lonely housewives in the more affluent areas of Toronto. With licence plates that read "MOTIV8TED" he was perfectly matched to his role as vice-president of business development.

Despite his popularity, it was hard to imagine people would even consider a cheesy snake like him to steer the Kudos ship. But from Kathryn's perspective, she felt she had a real fight on her hands.

Chapter 3 – Ready, Aim, Fire!

Day 1 – Morning Session

Fast-forward a couple of weeks and it was show time! The preparation blitz was a thing of the past. We had worked hard for twelve days, which felt like both a flash and a lifetime. Kathryn felt the odds were against her. The rate at which women moved into leadership roles at Kudos was glacial. Worst yet, Kathryn had not gained any momentum and the odds on heavy favourite Mr. Golden Boy Preston Steele had gone up. He was a master schmoozer with all the connections. He won support in a man's world through his sleazy wit, Colgate smile and non-stick armour. Shit didn't stick to this guy. If it was a boxing match, he would have been a 20 to 1 favourite!

Truth be told, Preston didn't consider Kathryn a serious contender. Kathryn heard through the grapevine that he had spread a rumour that she was the token female on the executive team. True to his style, he'd said Kathryn was there to get them all juiced up with her hot looks and high-heeled shoes. It was clear that Preston considered Kathryn a warm-up fight. He was already planning his next move into the CEO role and to boot her out of the running.

We sat with Kathryn in a large conference room on the twenty-second floor at Kudos. Tomorrow she would face executive hiring committee. It was time for the last dry run. All bets were pretty much up. Kathryn addressed the mock panel and was intense, slick, on a roll. She was ready.

Tomorrow the panel would be comprised of six people from the executive hiring committee: five from the organisation plus an external consultant they'd hired. The external consultant, Emma Darling, was from a reputable executive search firm. Her role was to legitimise the process and help with all the recruitment steps from the ground up.

We knew Emma Darling. She was, without a doubt, a piece of work. We had no idea why she'd been selected to be part of the committee. We thought it was perhaps because she was elegant and flashy and looked the part. The irony was that Emma's attraction to executive recruitment had everything to do with the money, power, and glory connected with networking with the who's who in Canadian business. It had nothing to do with helping clients.

You've met people like Emma before. People who are at the centre of their own universe. Her skill was building relationships that helped her get a leg up. Once your time was up, she'd forget you faster than a New York minute. For the Emmas of this world, people are dispensable, just a means to an end. It's nothing personal.

Knowing that Emma was like this made us nervous. We knew what an opportunist she was. Her modest background made her hungry for a better life. She was the type of woman who would sell her grandmother if she thought it would make her a few bucks. We were curious as to how she'd been presenting Kathryn to the hiring committee. She'd probably worked hard to make Kathryn feel like a star. Maybe sold her a line or two and pandered to her insecurities. She was good at that. Kathryn wouldn't have suspected a thing.

Kathryn and Preston were both candidates from Emma's executive search firm. Everyone knew Emma had a weakness for powerful, rich and good-looking men. We saw her loneliness and believed she'd give up just about everything for love. Hopefully she hadn't decided to back the person she viewed as the hottest prospect. We'd soon find out.

Kathryn had ninety minutes to present and defend her candidacy. Ninety minutes that, to Kathryn, felt like forever. She was determined. She was going to blow their socks off. Game on, people, it was show time!

She knew a huge part of her success lay in her ability to read her audience. She had to know the committee inside out, warts and all. Information equals power, and the only way she felt she could win this gig was to target their hot spots. She had to know their story – understand what made them tick. Not one to take any chances, she had put two of her best on the case full time. Tim and Ann were given carte blanche and a fat budget to dig up some dirt. No holds barred. Kathryn made it clear to her pumped-up team that she'd do whatever it took to win.

What Kathryn's team dug up on Emma left everybody speechless. Tim and Ann heard that she'd had the hots for Preston. They spent a few days waiting in the parking lot to follow her movements and see what she was up to. They staked her out for three days and came up with nothing. And then the unexpected happened. On the fourth day, Tim and Ann followed Emma to a fancy looking apartment in Yorkville. The doorman appeared to know her. It was clear this wasn't her first visit. A few hours later Emma emerged from the building with a man. It was Preston Steele! They watched as Preston pulled Emma closer towards him in a passionate kiss. He stroked her backside and lower back. This was not a professional visit. Emma was sleeping with the enemy.

CHAPTER 4 – BALLS THE SIZE OF GRAPEFRUITS

Later on Day 1 – No More Feeling Like a Doormat

The dry run was done. It had gone beautifully. We were back in Kathryn's office, going over a few details and reminiscing about the past. Her training was done. There was no point in going further. In fact, over preparing was the danger to avoid.

This was Kathryn second attempt to make a play for the head honcho job at Kudos. The first time she tried she'd cracked under the pressure. What hurt her was her need for approval from other people. She kept waiting on a sign from the top that she was seen as the right person for the job. As the days passed, the acknowledgement never came and the self-doubt gnawed away at her confidence until she melted into a puddle of nothing. It was self-fulfilling prophecy time and for a short time she did become a nothing person, forgettable and easy to miss.

We are not exactly sure of when the shift in her psyche happened, when she decided that enough was enough and that she was finally ready to play with the big boys and try to beat them at their own game.

We remember her bursting into our office; it must have been four of five years back, with a fiercely determined look in her eyes we'd never seen before. Her look said: "I've had enough of feeling like a doormat. I'm not taking any more shit from anyone!" She told us that from now on she would be the one with bigger balls and that she was going to take a swing at anyone who stood in her way. She said to us – and this is a direct quote – "I've got balls the size of grapefruits! If anybody has a problem with that, I'm not a hard woman to find."

We asked her if she could pinpoint a specific event that triggered her change. She wasn't sure and neither were we. Frankly, we don't think she cared about how it happened. She was moving at the speed of light with little regard for consequences and a tunnel-vision focus on the main prize.

As business hours were long over, Kathryn opened a bottle of red wine and poured us all a glass. She needed to unwind. She deserved it. We talked some more and listened to her that night. It occurred us that she had gone from practicing a combat sport just for fun, to wanting to go pro and be the best. She used to be someone we would have described as having talent and a few flashy moves, but now she had her training wheels off and she was ready to get into the ring and fight for real.

But we were still not sure if she could pull it off. Her self-esteem was still pretty shaky. Despite all the hot air, we knew her armour was not bulletproof. If she failed, she would need a lot of support. We would be ready either way.

CHAPTER 5 – BACKFIRE

Day 2 – 7:30 a.m.

This was the day. The day that would make or break Kathryn's shot at the title. Her interview was at 4:45 p.m. sharp. Preston Steele's was on immediately after hers.

Kathryn was in a foul mood. Tim and Ann had told her about Emma and Preston. Kathryn was in shock but wanted to play it cool and give Emma a chance to do the right thing. She wanted to see just how far Emma would continue playing the game before she revealed to Emma that she knew her secret.

In their meeting, Emma paid Kathryn lip service. She gave the standard platitudes: that the CEO's job was not the be all and end all, how she had every right to be proud of her performance so far, and – wait for it – that whatever happened, she had a great future ahead. It made Kathryn sick to her stomach to hear Emma preparing her for defeat. Knowing Emma was screwing Preston and watching Emma lie to her face was a bitter pill to swallow.

She had been counting on Emma to be her ally and had buttered her up over the last few weeks, promising her a truckload of business. Kathryn had been screwed over by Emma and was furious. She was going to take her down.

"So, Emma, how's Preston's campaign going?" Kathryn asked. "I'm really relying on you to provide both of us with different ways in which we can present ourselves in the best possible light and secure the position based on who is better equipped for the role. What are your instincts so far? Who do you think is going to make it?"

Kathryn watched as Emma shifted uncomfortably in her seat. "You are both really neck and neck in this. Very different. It just depends on what the board is looking for. I'm not sure what else to tell you, Kathryn." Emma spoke in a quiet voice and dropped her gaze.

"Are you sure you've told me everything Emma? You know our relationship has got to be completely transparent. As my advisor, I am relying on you to help me make the right decisions," Kathryn told her.

Emma did not answer.

"Nothing to say Emma?" Kathryn glared at her, refusing to avert her steely gaze.

"Nothing more than I shared already, Kathryn," she whispered.

"Well, we both know that's not true," said Kathryn. "When were you going to tell me that you've been banging Preston?"

Emma went silent.

"Get out of my sight Emma! I don't have to tell you what this means for your career. I am going to have to insist that your remove yourself from the selection panel and notify the committee of your conflict of interest. As for me, I haven't decided yet how to make you useful to me. One thing's for sure, I want to know everything you have said about me to Preston. I want to know what you've shared with the panel that could have corrupted their view of me in your efforts to give Preston the edge over me." Kathryn was fuming. "Now leave please. I can't even bear to look at you right now. You make me sick!"

Emma looked grief stricken and scurried away, her face streaming with the crocodile tears of a person who had been found out.

We didn't dare ask Kathryn if she had been expecting some kind of collegial female solidarity. We knew the answer to that one. Kathryn had a long history of not getting on too well with other women. There had never been such thing as a real and legit girls' club in her professional life. Kathryn's personal belief was that women in power only knew one thing, how to double cross and stab each other in the back. It was a major source of frustration for her in our sessions. She slumped in her chair and told us that she felt like a fool for thinking it would be any different this time around. We knew Kathryn's tendency to tar all women with the same brush would only exacerbate her feelings of betrayal. In fairness, Kathryn should have been more on the ball and recognised Emma for who she was. She hadn't read the play and now it was probably going to bite her in the backside.

Even with Emma forced out of the picture, it was hard to know what damage had already been done to her reputation. She needed to find out. The sand in the hourglass was almost out.

Kathryn was incredibly distracted after her run in with Emma. We needed to get her back on track and asked her to describe how the meeting with Emma had gone in more detail. She shared snippets of the conversation and told us she'd really busted out the heavy artillery. She was not going to lie down quietly. She had dug up enough dirt on Emma to force her to keep a low profile and even the playing field. Emma didn't really have a choice. She had to agree to Kathryn's terms and conditions and was thrown out on her arse.

Time would only tell how much permanent damage Emma's undermining had done in the last month. We cautioned Kathryn and advised her to move through her anger and betrayal as quickly as possible. She wanted Emma's blood and had no desire to show mercy.

When push came to shove, we understood that Emma's behaviour wasn't about Kathryn at all. It wasn't personal. For Emma, it all boiled down to her gaining favour with the object of her affections in the hope of finding true love. It had backfired on her.

With Emma out of the picture, we needed a new game plan. Kathryn had to come up with a new strategy to become top dog and fast.

CHAPTER 6 – KEEPING IT REAL

Day 2 - 8:30 a.m.

We needed to take some time out from all the political antics and refocus. When it was all said and done, there was one simple truth. Kathryn was the better candidate for the CEO role. There was no question. We knew it, but did she believe it? We set out to prove it. Here's what we came up with:

1. **Business sense.** Kathryn has a better and broader understanding of Kudos' business than Preston. Preston has street-smarts credibility, but he is clueless about almost everything else. He is strictly an operations guy, focused on ensuring his people get stuff done and so he can look good. Kathryn is more well-rounded, a blue-sky thinker with loads of substance.

2. **Vision.** Kathryn has a daring and innovative vision for Kudos. New technologies will transform the way Kudos does business. It will reinvigorate their main revenue streams. She knows it and she's prepared for it. Creativity runs through her veins. She's capable of taking this business to a whole other level.

3. **Leadership.** Kathryn is an outstanding leader. She is humble and leads by example. Her track record speaks for itself. Building powerful and effective teams is second nature to her – period.

4. **Enthusiasm.** Kathryn is dedicated and hungry, more so than anyone else on the executive team. Her desire to win and take the company into another stratosphere is unparalleled. This is what she does. This is who she is.

5. **Track record.** Kathryn knows how to streamline costs and turn Kudos into a well-oiled machine. She's done it before with all her departments. She can do it again. These are the facts, and she's got the numbers to prove it.

Kathryn has the goods. She's focussed, is clear in where she wants to take Kudos, and has the data to back up every claim she makes. She's got depth. Putting her into the top job makes sense. This begs the question, why is Preston even in the running?

Preston has the edge on two counts. Firstly, he looks the part. From all accounts he is an average leader, nothing special at all. But damn, is he slick! He says all the right things and people love him. He's a pimped out leader on steroids and he's got everybody fooled.

Preston is also hyper-connected. He's a master networker and friends with all the who's who. Rumour has it he has the skinny on many of his powerful friends, and that makes him dangerous and untouchable.

As lunchtime approached, we remained silent for a while. It was pretty clear that it was not a moral victory that Kathryn was aiming for. There were no prizes for coming in second. Kathryn was not going to take solace from impressing the committee in a losing effort. She was the best candidate and she wanted to win. She was convinced she could pull it off.

Chapter 7 – Tapped Out

Day 2 – Noon

Kathryn was in a room nearby having a quick bite with her husband Bruce. We could hear her through the paper-thin walls – she was not a happy camper. Bruce tried to calm her down but it didn't work. Bruce did his best to offer support, but he said all the wrong things. Kathryn was irate, but in fairness to poor old Bruce, she was too on edge to hear anyone.

It was no surprise that Bruce's efforts to console his wife were near useless. He was a good guy, but on the emotional intelligence scale he was a zero. He didn't get her. He hadn't for a long time now. He had no idea how much his wife had changed. Kathryn wouldn't allow herself to be second best anymore. Her fighting spirit had raised her from sleepwalking through work to striving for more. She was a fighter now. No more apologies. No more asking for permission. She had reprogrammed herself for success. Kathryn was ready to tap out Preston Steele.

We felt sorry for Bruce. There wasn't a lot he could do to help her except reassure her and tell her that everything would go well. He reminded her that she already had a good job and a great life with him.

"You've got nothing to lose babe, it doesn't matter if you don't get the job. Just give it your best shot!" he told her lovingly.

We were surprised Kathryn didn't knock Bruce out after that. Instead, she went quiet. She loved her husband but she knew he had no backbone for fighting. We're pretty sure Kathryn had already mentally checked out and was preserving her energy for the real showdown. She was anxious to finish her lunch and get back into the ring.

A few minutes later we saw them in the hallway. Bruce wished her good luck and told her that he loved her. She mumbled something back. She was far away – no longer interested in being the loving wife and mother. She was focussed on one thing and one thing only: beating Preston Steele.

Chapter 8 – Talk is Cheap

Day 2 – Early Afternoon

We waited in a small meeting room. Kathryn's two main advisors burst in with an update and all hell broke loose. The word on the street was that Emma Darling was back at it. She'd been spreading rumours that Kathryn was not a good enough people-leader for the CEO gig. Emma said that Kathryn was not someone who could galvanise the troops beyond her inner circle. She said Kathryn alienated people.

The extent of Emma's treachery finally hit home. Preston was not the bad guy here. Preston was not even Kathryn's biggest adversary. It was Emma Darling, conspiring and plotting Kathryn's demise just to please her boyfriend. At the end of the day… it's all about sex.

Kathryn now realized she would probably not get this job. And it wasn't because of a sleazy salesman like Preston, or a male-dominated company culture or even because she was a woman. She had been fighting an invisible force. She'd been up against a nasty woman with her own personal agenda who was determined to destroy Kathryn for her own gain.

Then someone who claimed to have seen the results of Kathryn's psychometric testing leaked out a story that gave legs to Emma's fabrications about Kathryn. Along similar lines, Preston was held to be the better candidate because he tested well as an inspiring leader. This was absolute crap, but the gossip was out of control. It weakened Kathryn's position.

You've got to hand it to Emma. Her ability to spread toxicity about Kathryn was like an untreated cancer that had taken over Kudos.

We know that the power of false rumours and constructed realities cannot be underestimated. In our combined thirty years of experience as executive coaches, we've seen far too many times how fabricated lies and gossip can destroy careers in a nanosecond. We knew that we could not waste a moment. It was time to get into a huddle and tweak our game plan. Even if Kathryn didn't stand a strong chance, she would not go down without a fight.

- **Strategy 1** – There was no room for defensiveness. Our first strategy was to remind Kathryn that she should not under any circumstances appear defensive during her presentation. She had to be the duck gliding on the pond while paddling furiously underneath the surface. Cool, poised and collected. Bitterness never wins any points.

- **Strategy 2** – Talk about the elephant in the room. We advised Kathryn to raise the leadership reputation gossip right from the get go. There was no sense in waiting. We already knew what everyone had heard. She needed to flag it and address it. Better to nip the sucker in the bud and clear their attention to focus on the good stuff.
- **Strategy 3** – Don't reveal the relationship between Emma and Preston. Women who lash out publically at other women end up getting punished. Better to force Emma to withdraw from the process and fess up to what she had done herself rather than talk about it. We were all in agreement. If we played it like this, chances were we had a shot at being able to turn the rumours to our advantage. We needed a good angle though.
- **Strategy 4** – Don't play the woman card. We advised Kathryn to argue that Kudos Industries had never seen leadership like hers before but not mention gender. Kudos needed a sea of change to reinvigorate the business. Her plan? To work with the business to create think tanks to gather up the best ideas from the floor and act on them. Kathryn was going to share her ideas on how she would empower people at all levels to unleash their creativity and enhance business performance.
- **Strategy 5** – Inspire the committee with her vision of what the organisation would look like with her at the helm. Kathryn's goal was to transform Kudos' unhealthy corporate culture to become constructive and a great place to work. Her closing statement had us all inspired. Her new vision of the Kudos world meant that all employees were viewed as leaders and encouraged to take personal responsibility for creating the new culture at Kudos as a great place to work. "It's what the company needs," she was going to say. "The time is now and I am the person to make it happen."

The mood in the meeting room was remarkably intense at this point. We were all staring at Kathryn. We knew she was the best candidate for the role, but we were concerned that her stunning pitch would not strike the right chord for all the committee members.

Someone – perhaps Ann, one of Kathryn's main advisors – had a brilliant idea. She proposed that Kathryn do the unexpected and actually demonstrate "live" how her team leadership was really first-rate by inviting direct reports into the presentation to give their views on Kathryn as a leader. Let the committee decide for themselves. We were all sold on the idea. Let's face it, with the stakes so high we had everything to gain and nothing to lose.

CHAPTER 9 – LEATHER WHIPS AND CHAINS

Day 2 – 3:15 p.m.

The mood flipped from psyched up to sombre. Bob, Kathryn's sad sack of a mentor, showed up and from all indications things didn't look good. He told us that it was unlikely that the majority would vote for Kathryn. Talk about raining on her parade. Now was not the time to threaten Kathryn's positive psyche. It felt like a deliberate attempt to throw her off her game. She already knew where things were at and didn't need to be thrown any more rotten eggs.

We pulled him to one side and gave him the hard word.

"Look Bob, we appreciate your insights, but what would really help Kathryn right now is some information on who's in that room. Tell Kathryn everything she needs to know to have greater impact. Help her or leave." We pointed at the doorway.

"Well," he said, taking a deep breath, "there's Mr. Rosenberg. He's the oldest guy on the committee. He retired from corporate life a few years back, but keeps hanging around to give his life some semblance of a purpose between golf games. He's been with Kudos forever. But don't waste your time with him, he's a lost cause. Plus, he and Preston are really tight. At best, he'll be pleasantly surprised by Kathryn's presentation because Preston and Emma have set the bar on Kathryn pretty low." He turned to Kathryn. "He's the kind of old fart to tell you as much."

So could Kathryn do enough to change his vote? No way.

1-0 Preston.

Bob continued on, sneering. "Then there's Mrs. Susan White. She's an old-school Kudos veteran. She scratched and clawed her way to the top and was the first woman to make it onto the executive team just as a VP Human Resources, but still. I know she's got a good relationship with Preston too. She's also got the reputation for blocking other women climbing too far up the ladder. I think it's because she gets off on being a queen bee way too much to share the spotlight. I tried to get a sense from her as to whether she was pro Kathryn or not, but she froze me out."

What we found out later was that Kathryn was being informally mentored by Susan White. Susan had reluctantly agreed to work with Kathryn to try and tear down her reputation as being a vicious she-male with no heart. But Susan didn't really want Kathryn to get the job. She felt it would threaten her position on the executive team and she didn't want to compete.

Instead, she spent her session putting Kathryn down with criticism and blame. Years later, Kathryn admitted to feeling beat up every time she had a session with Susan. We found out that Susan hadn't defended the rumours about Kathryn either, even though she knew they weren't true. She didn't want to get involved.

2-0 Preston.

Bob kept on with the run down. Our hopes still rested in the three remaining committee members – Mr. Faris, Mr. Levine and Ms. Huffington.

Over the past few weeks, we had helped Kathryn tailor specific parts of her presentation to appeal to all the committee members in some way. Perhaps there was a glimmer of hope. Alas, good old Bob was a party killer since he'd just gotten word that Ms. Huffington was now on the Preston bandwagon and Mr. Levine was on the fence. That slimy bastard had canoodled his way in yet again. Maybe he was screwing her too.

Truth be told, Mr. Faris was the only one who was really in Kathryn's corner. He was an old friend of the Stringers and a very clever man. He had seen right through Preston's charm and knew that new blood was what Kudos needed to reinvent itself. Besides, he and Kathryn did have a history of sorts. He had originally hired her way back in the day. He had been a fan ever since, very discreetly, but a fan nonetheless.

Bob sighed heavily again, his whole demeanour sweating defeat. We had to get him out of there before he proposed surrender. If he did we were ready to lynch him but he didn't get the chance. Kathryn cut him off and put us all out of our misery.

"Enough!" she said. "I have heard enough. Bob's predictions may be based on fair assumptions but it's beside the point. If I thought like that, I wouldn't have moved up from middle management. When you think like a loser, you become one! I'm done with all this loser talk. Bob, get out!" She pointed at the door as he quietly exited.

We really admired Kathryn. Her transformation from doormat to warrior has been impressive. She refused to believe that there was no way to change the mind of old man Rosenberg and the rest of them. She was not about to find reasons to lose.

The reality was that deep down Kathryn knew she was the better candidate. She just had to try to find a way to convince the committee she was the only choice, notwithstanding Emma's poisoning.

"If they can't see it, it's up to me to open their eyes" she said with determination. "If they're scared, it's up to me to reassure them. If they are not ready for me, I'll find a way to show them the door. It's my time to shine!"

Kathryn was smiling and eager to get in the room. One way or an other, a decision had to be made and she was tired of waiting.

Tim proposed that Kathryn show up to the presentation with "a big-arse leather whip to beat the committee into submission." Everyone laughed. The mood in the room had lifted. We were ready to win. There was no room for negative naysayers at this stage of the game.

Chapter 10 - It's Showtime

Day 2 – 4:35 p.m.

Kathryn dressed herself for power and impact that day. Her new designer red crepe suit contrasted beautifully against the silk cream shirt that showed off just enough cleavage without being too provocative. Her long auburn hair fell naturally down her back which gave her a much more relaxed and quietly confident demeanour than the usual tightly pulled-back French braid.

The presentation was about to start. With ten minutes to go, we rounded out the last minute details. Kathryn was calm, she knew her stuff and she looked spectacular. Tim went over all the key points one last time. He'd arranged for the entire team to show up in the last twenty minutes of the presentation. They were going to talk about Kathryn's leadership skills and hammer home how awesome she was.

We looked over and saw Ann in the corner of the room discreetly working on a concession speech. She winked at us. It was her job to prepare for every eventuality and there were a few scenarios left to consider. We weren't really sure what tack Kathryn would end up taking, but we figured she had about three potential options. One: she could right out quit. And let's face it, no-one would blame her given the dog and pony show she was being asked to give. Two: she could bow out gracefully and take some time off. Three: she could leverage the committee's guilt into her preferred position. Kathryn didn't let on what she had decided to do.

There was a knock at the door. Somebody showed up to announce the committee was ready and Kathryn had to leave right away. At this point we still thought we had a shot, but it was a long shot. There was no doubt in our minds that Kathryn would make a very powerful CEO. There was no doubt she was ready for it. We knew that to have a female CEO in a male dominated environment would buck existing trends and reinvigorate the organisation. Kathryn was fighting against institutional barriers and entrenched social norms – it would be a miracle if she could tear down those walls and start to turn the tides at Kudos.

If she lost, we bet our money on her quitting straight away. Too much was on the line now. There was no way she could stay on and play second fiddle to Preston Steele. Not in this lifetime. Kathryn put on her jacket and jumped toward the door. She was psyched and in the zone. All bets were off now.

She casually strolled into the meeting room and stood at the head of the boardroom table and began: "Good afternoon, everyone. Thank you for the opportunity to be considered to be the new leader of Kudos. I am deeply honoured. I hope that in the next hour I will be able to demonstrate to you why I am the right choice to lead Kudos into the future."

Chapter 11 – Rollercoaster Ride

Day 2 – 6:30 p.m.

It was a thing of beauty. Everything went perfectly and according to plan. Kathryn's presentation was stunning, pure poetry in motion. Kathryn was on. The core of her speech, the piece around her vision for the company, blew everyone away. She had everyone transfixed. She delivered her punchlines flawlessly. Hell, we felt like running out of the room to go buy shares in the company!

The inspired energy that permeated the room when Kathryn's team walked in was transcendent. And, for twenty minutes or so, we heard some very open and genuine experiences of what it was like to work with her.

It was a great mix of story-telling, anecdotes, a few well delivered self-deprecating jokes and some heartfelt moments. It was a raw and authentic plea for more from a bunch of talented people thriving under Kathryn's leadership. She was poised for greatness and ready for success. Kathryn presented herself well. She came across as an engaging and empowering people leader – as a visionary who sets a clear direction while leveraging her team's strengths to the max.

Kathryn surprised us all by pulling a final white rabbit out of the hat. She went completely off script and talked about the deficit of women in leadership positions at Kudos. She spoke passionately about the glass ceiling that remains pervasive, and how hard it was to try and succeed in that world. She told the hiring committee how she had always had to work harder than her male colleagues to get noticed and how stressful it was to always have to be better, stronger and faster to get ahead.

"I don't want my gender to be an issue in your decision" Kathryn told them. "I want to be rewarded the job for being myself, for being seen by you as having the greatest potential. Because you see me as the best leader for the Kudos' future," she implored.

There was a long, silent pause. Kathryn stopped speaking for what felt like a very long time. We all started to get a little nervous, not knowing what was coming next. There wasn't much time left. Was that a wrap? And then she did it. She had left the best until last. One by one she walked over to each member of the committee, looked them straight in the eye and spoke to them directly.

Her closing argument put her at great personal risk but she went for it anyway. The first person she addressed was Mrs. White.

"Mrs. White, you have the reputation of not helping other women out. We have both had our differences in the past. But it's time for change. Let another woman sit at the table beside you. I'd like that woman to be me," she said sincerely.

Next up was Mr. Rosenberg.

"Mr. Rosenberg, how would you feel about being led by a woman? Be honest," she insisted. "What about by a sexy woman with way more power than you? Could you see yourself submitting and towing the party line? How would that feel for you Mr. Rosenberg?"

We didn't know how far she was going to get with this line of questioning but we admired her for her bravery. And then she delivered the home run.

"At the end of the day, me becoming CEO should not be about fears of female domination and power struggles. I know how to bring people together. I know how to get them to focus on Kudos' mission and value proposition and drive us to greatness."

Everyone in the room was blown away by her candour and conviction. Old Rosenberg was shaking like a leaf. We figured he had soiled his pants thinking she had made it and won everybody over. Kathryn had given an unbelievable performance. She had taken a big risk presenting with such frankness, but it could still go either way.

CHAPTER 12 – A WOLF IN SHEEP'S CLOTHING

Day 2 – 7:30 p.m.

Preston had been stealthily planning his attack for weeks. Emma had of course been incredibly useful. She'd given him the down-low of Kathryn's vulnerabilities and he was ready to stick the knife in. He was continually amazed at how the power of pillow talk had given him the edge in his career.

After all, it was Peter Stringer's wife that had really paved the way for him at Kudos. He'd met her one Friday afternoon having drinks at Ki, a funky modern Japanese bar and eatery in Toronto's financial district. He had no idea who she was at first and had just taken her for one of the regular bar stars that hung out at high-end establishments after work to try and pick up rich, eligible men. She played right into his hands. She was like most wives of the powerful men that he knew, over-processed, lonely as hell, and hiding a messy drinking problem.

The affair lasted as long as it took him to get the job at Kudos – all of five minutes. Delilah had convinced her husband that Kudos needed a business development gun like him to help them increase market share. His network of A-list connections made him a more attractive proposition for Peter who wasn't much into socialising and was happy to pass this on to Preston to make sure they were talking to all the right people.

Delilah supported Preston's decision to make a play for her husband's job. It was her way of appeasing him so he wouldn't blow the lid on her infidelity. Part of the deal was that she would give him insider information on her family's plans to build the intangible value of Kudos to position it for an eventual sale. She shared with him the hot buttons to push to get the other members of the executive on his side, she told him how to engage every board member and what to say to impress her husband Peter and his father Cornelius.

Preston's presentation hit the mark. It didn't matter that he didn't have a proven track record of success or that he'd only been with the company for less than a year. He played right into their hands and they loved what they heard. Many of the board members commented later about how incredible it was how he nailed their vision for the future. Preston was seen as a genius.

Chapter 13 – Who's Your Daddy

Day 2 - 8:15 p.m.

Back in the green room, the mood was manic. We all believed that Kathryn still had a shot for the CEO title. We had no idea what Preston had been up to or Delilah's involvement in all this. Had we known, we would have advised her very differently.

Amidst all the high-fiving and gushing over Kathryn, people were trying to get the inside scoop on how she'd done. We were wondering whether the committee would deliberate all night, or take their time and prolong the suspense. Maybe they'd call the candidates back for a second round of questioning. It was hard to say.

Then a bomb went off. We got wind that Preston had gone way over time in his presentation – which was technically not allowed. We also heard that he talked at length about Kathryn. We heard from someone inside who claimed to have seen an early version of Preston's speech and swore to us it was very complimentary of Kathryn. We thought that this was all part of his master game plan. Show someone close to Kathryn a positive version of everything he would say about her and then, turn on her behind closed doors.

Preston's strategy paid off. The news came in. Preston Steele was the new CEO of Kudos. It had been a fait accompli. We felt heavy and deflated, as if the air had been sucked out of the room.

We still didn't know how much Emma's wicked manipulating had played a role in Kathryn's defeat. But we weren't naïve enough to think that anyone couldn't have been negatively skewed by the filth she had spewed about Kathryn. We knew that Mrs. White had also remained a passive resistor. She had the opportunity to defend Kathryn's reputation but didn't. As far as we were concerned she was as much to blame as Emma for orchestrating Kathryn's inevitable defeat.

Chapter 14 – The Disappearance of Kathryn

It had been six weeks since Kathryn lost out to Preston. She was nowhere to be found. Nobody had seen her. Inside sources told us she had hopped on a plane that same night and flew by herself to an undisclosed location, somewhere far away in the sun. Rumour had it she had probably drank herself into oblivion and passed out somewhere under a palm tree.

Kathryn had sent in her resignation first thing the next morning. Preston did not accept it at first, convinced she would come to her senses and come back. Her departure had him spooked. He had counted on her to still be there. He had crafted a huge "I need you – I can't do this without you" speech, which was in fact true. He had planned to delegate the job to her while he took all the credit for the company's success. But Kathryn didn't bite.

He offered her everything but the keys to the castle – more status, money, perks – the whole nine yards, but there was nothing he could do to convince her to stay.

Her reply was short and to the point. "You've got to be kidding, Preston," she scoffed. "With everything that I know about you? I hope you choke on it."

Her supporters were still chuckling about her response weeks after she left.

The Board had underestimated her too. They knew what they had in her, but never thought they would lose her. They figured she'd be like most other women, grateful for still having a well-paid position and understanding of the fact that she's lost out to a candidate better suited to the CEO position than her.

It didn't take long for them to realise that in Preston they had a good-looking sack of nothing. He didn't have the goods to be the new CEO of Kudos. But it was too late; Kathryn had vanished and Kudos began to internally combust. Without Kathryn's vision, ability to manage innovation and skills in execution, Kudos was left vulnerable to external forces and the outdated thinking of its founders.

Chapter 15 – Dark Shadows

Kathryn kept us all guessing. We didn't know where she'd gone and we were worried about her. To go from flying so close to the sun, to a monumental crash landing had to have been devastating even for a warrior princess like Kathryn.

The fact of the matter was that Kathryn had managed perceptions of her departure with great cunning. Her decision to leave had left Kudos' godfathers shell-shocked. They wiped her off as foolish, believing that her female emotions had gotten in the way of her making the right and rational decision. Secretly, they respected her more than ever.

The truth was that Kathryn had hit rock bottom. The stress of all the lies, the undermining antics, the bullying and the Stringer family drama had finally taken its toll and Kathryn was emotionally spent.

In her heart of hearts, her idealistic self always believed that in the end the best person for the job would succeed and justice would prevail. To accept that she has been upstaged by an imposter like Preston was more than she could bear. It really was a man's world, a world in which she believed was always going to be an uneven playing field.

Kathryn spent close to one year hiding out from her corporate life at her lake house in Muskoka. It was an idyllic spot. A quaint log cottage surrounded by bursts of brightly coloured rhododendrons and a green mirrored lake. This had always been her sanctuary, the one place she could find peace. Not even poor old Bruce could break through the 10-foot wall she had built around herself.

What irked Kathryn the most were the lengths that Emma had gone to in order to sabotage her career. And she did it all for the occasional romp with a cad like Preston. She couldn't understand how anyone could be so cruel and vindictive. Then there was her mentor, Mrs. White. She had every opportunity to save Kathryn's reputation and hadn't even tried. Kathryn felt she had been damned from every angle.

Perhaps it was the quiet achievers that deliver the goods who make it to the top in the end. The fact that she hadn't made it was a reality she couldn't accept.

The incredible disillusionment and feelings of betrayal sent her spiralling down tunnel of darkness and the black dog barked so loudly that it blinded her to any glimmers of hope. She had always thought of herself as strong and together. Yet here she was, feeling kicked to the curb with no energy to fight back.

Months later, Kathryn had called Jean-François and asked him to come see her. He could hear it in her voice. She was displaying all the signs of someone who was suffering from the silent epidemic we had encountered so many times before, that of someone who had been repeatedly pushed around at work. The cumulative impact of Emma's undermining her abilities and character assassination coupled with Mrs. White's blatant lack of support and underlying bullying, plus years of being blocked from career opportunities, had taken its toll. This once-powerful woman who didn't take crap from anyone had melted into a puddle.

Kathryn was like many who suffer emotional abuse at work; she didn't know it was happening. She had found several reasons to rationalise the bullying. She passed it off as bad behaviour or as someone having a crappy day.

We understood the extent of the damage. We also knew that for women bullied by other women, the psychological trauma tends to be felt a lot more deeply. Kathryn had experienced it from all sides. From men she almost expected it. But from other women? She had expected better from them. Weren't they supposed to help her? Women were already so under-represented in leadership roles, surely it was up to women in positions of power to part the Red Sea as much as possible, to help increase female representation at the top?

Jean-François helped Kathryn come to terms with what had happened to her. Naming the pain was the first step and a day of liberation. She became aware of how her self-esteem had been eroding with every new attack until she had folded.

As the days passed, Kathryn worked through her shock and anger to accept the reality of what she'd experienced. It wasn't just about having to navigate her way through a man's world of work, it was also about coming to terms with the fact that if she wanted to get back into the ring, she needed to be more astute about her adversaries and her supporters, male and female. She needed to be better prepared than she had been. Her naiveté had clouded her judgment.

Through her desire to fight back, Kathryn found renewed strength and purpose. Almost two years later, like a phoenix rising from the ashes, Kathryn dusted the dirt from her wings and prepared to return to the jungle.

Chapter 16 – Divine Retribution

Kudos had once ruled the gaming industry. Now it was now but a shadow of its former self. With the steady demise of the organisation under the rule of a puppet, Peter Stringer had his father Cornelius step in to try and save their life's work from complete extinction.

We heard from Kathryn that they had tried to contact her and left messages on her cell phone begging her to return. She would never go back.

Shortly after she lost out to Preston, Kathryn heard from the owner of Joker Inc. Joker had always played second fiddle to Kudos. When they heard that Kudos had let the brains behind their innovations go, and that Kathryn was back in town, they wooed her relentlessly. Exactly one year 11 months and 20 days after she walked out of Kudos, Kathryn became the new COO of Joker.

As for Kudos, the market showed its lack of faith in CEO Preston Steele, and their stocks' value plummeted. Kudos was a vulnerable enterprise that was ripe for a takeover. Now Joker Inc. dominated the gaming industry with their latest product developments and pioneering mindset. Behind closed doors, the Board of Kudos and Joker had made a decision to merge and save what was left of the company. Even the Stringers were kept out of the deal. Their inability to keep their own personal issues out of the business had cost Kudos way too much and the Board still hadn't figured out how or what to do with them. The deal was completed with Joker having 51% of the shares of Kudos. Things were finally about to change.

It was late September when Kudos called a press conference with all of its stakeholders and the media. We were invited to attend. Kudos' chairman, Walter Strozzaprezzi, looked nervous as he made his way up to the podium. Kudos had received a hell of a lot of bad press about its plummeting share prices and we were expecting bad news.

Looking very GQ, Walter stood up in his navy-blue pinstriped suit and monogrammed cufflinks and made his announcement. "Welcome everyone. Thanks for coming today. I am sure you are all wondering why we have called you all here." He sounded quite agitated.

We were all getting ready to get the tissues out, thinking the worst. We thought it was strange that there wasn't a Stringer in sight.

"Today marks a momentous day in Kudos history. As you know, we haven't been doing too well lately. But we've decided to turn things around. We've had our butts kicked by Joker Inc. for long enough. We've decided if you can't beat 'em, join 'em. We will be joining forces and becoming one with Joker."

We were stunned by his announcement. The room went silent. After the initial shock, we couldn't help but feel relieved that Kudos wasn't going down the toilet.

Walter could see by the stunned looks on our faces that we were taken aback by the news.

"I can see many of you were not expecting this. But we are really excited about Kudos becoming part of the Joker family. And on a more personal note, we are thrilled to make another important announcement."

Yet another announcement? You could have heard a pin drop.

"Ladies and gentlemen, it took a lot of persuading; however, we are now thrilled to welcome the new CEO of Joker Inc., Kathryn Underwood!"

A breathtaking flame-haired Kathryn stepped up on the stage, her piercing blue eyes beaming with pride.

Walter continued to honour her. "Kathryn is the reason why Joker has singlehandedly taken over the market with its latest product innovations. Ladies and gentlemen, give it up for Kathryn Underwood!"

Kathryn walked over to the podium. "Thanks, Walter. Thanks, everyone. I am sure for many of you this has come as a huge shock. I must admit I even surprised myself when I decided to take on this role. But the offer was too good to pass up, and I am ready. I learned a lot about myself in the last few years, about the kind of leader I want to be, about how I want to be remembered. They say that we learn the most from failure. Well, my failures have made me better, wiser, and stronger. I am reinvigorated by the challenge to lead the new Joker into a future that knows no limits. Thank you!"

The audience stood, applauded and cheered.

Now that's what we call divine retribution.

PART TWO

Reality Check

Chapter 17 – It's a Man's World

America has forged this success while utilizing, in large part, only half of the country's talent. For most of our history, women – whatever their abilities – have been relegated to the sidelines. Only in recent years have we begun to correct that problem. – Warren Buffett

Kathryn's experiences at Kudos starkly reflect a current reality. As much as we would like to believe women have made progress in the workforce, discrimination is still very much alive and kicking. The vigorous debates started by Sheryl Sandberg (with her book Lean In: Women, Work And The Will To Lead) and many others like her herald the fact that gender related bias still exists.

So, as much as we wish things were different and some would like to believe that the problem has been corrected, the fact of the matter is that men still rule the world.

To illustrate, in the US men run roughly 97% of the largest public companies, hold 84% of major board positions and control 83% of Congress[1]. Women in power are a minority and tend to occupy lower status positions[2]. In Australia, the movement of women into senior leadership roles is reaching new global heights and can best be described as glacial[3]. In Canada, women hold 8.5 per cent of the highest-paid positions in Canada's top 100 listed companies, according a report by global executive search firm Rosenzweig & Company. That's almost double the 4.6 per cent recorded in 2006, the first year Rosenzweig studied women in executive positions, and up from 7.4 per cent in 2011.

The perennial glass ceiling remains a steadfast institutional barrier. Gender discrimination, unappealing stereotypes and the lack of support for motherhood also mean that women are less likely to make a play for more coveted roles, seeing defeat as imminent.

The under-representation of women at the upper echelons of business is not a new story, yet it is even harder to believe when we know that organisations that hire women into senior positions perform way better financially. Quite simply, placing women into strategic roles makes better business sense, end of story.

---

1   Goudreau, J. "Why Successful Women Terrify Us." Forbes Magazine (2012).
2   Eagly, A.H., & Carli, L. L. Through the Labyrinth: The Truth About How Women Become Leaders. Boston, MA: Harvard Business School Press, 2007.
3   Women's Workforce Representation: A Statistical Profile. EOWA (2008).

So, just how are women like Kathryn being rewarded for their contributions? In terms of salary, men and women still differ substantially in terms of pay, with the world salary gap between the sexes at 15.6% at the time of writing. In terms of promotions, women receive promotions less frequently than men and are even less likely to move into more senior roles. Case in point: we know that Kathryn would have made 20% less than Preston to become CEO of Kudos.

For Kathryn, the glass ceiling at Kudos unequivocally blocked her rise in the organisation. Equally, other barriers such as the very male-oriented organisational culture, a lack of access to high quality and interested mentors hurt her ability to acquire the level of organisational sponsorship she needed to secure a position at the executive table.

It is our belief that Kathryn's personality transformation from doormat to "bad ass" did not help her cause either. From a psychological perspective we know that neither ends of the spectrum would create a favourable impression of a female leader wanting to enhance her career.

Researchers call this phenomenon the double-bind effect. Also known as the backlash effect[4], it is defined as the social and economic reprisals for behaving counter stereotypically. To counteract its effects, women must become more conscious of it and seek to proactively manage it. So as an example, acting like a guy at work does women a disservice.

But avoiding this catch-22 situation is easier said than done. Because women don't typically have the same access to higher level leadership opportunities, they often feel compelled to engage in behaviours that are perceived as unwomanly. They become loudly vocal about their accomplishments, they are perceived as too ambitious because they've dared to ask for a salary increase, or they are seen as aggressive when being assertive. These actions cause them to be viewed negatively by both men and women alike. It's a case of damned if you do and damned if you don't. Kathryn's sudden evolution into an aggressive, gun-toting cowgirl with testicular fortitude[5] probably eroded her reputation as an easy-going high achiever, and weakened her candidacy for the CEO role at Kudos.

It doesn't stop there. There is strong evidence to demonstrate that women viewed as powerful are often perceived as intimidating, abnormal, and unattractive. A recent article in the New York Times shared interviews with four executives on succeeding in business as women. There was a strong

---

4   Rudman, L.A., Phelan, J. E. "Backlash Effects for Disconfirming Gender Stereotypes in Organizations." *Research in Organizational Behaviour* (2008), 28, 68-79.

5   Isaac, C. (2012) The next generation of female leaders will emerge at a faster pace when women stop trying to 'act like men'. Forbes Woman

message that many women won't ask for what they want, for fear of their strong leadership becoming synonymous with negative labels like aggressive, controlling and demanding or, God forbid, being ascribed the dreaded bitch label[6].

There's no doubt that women leaders are susceptible to unfair prejudice and labels. To realise the extent of it can be shocking to say the least. To illustrate, we'd like to share the story of one of our colleagues, Sylvie. Her experience is worth sharing as it heralded a major tipping point in her own leadership evolution that we can all learn from.

The Lockout that Rocked a Nation

On August 15, 2005, almost 90% percent of CBC/Radio Canada employees were locked out by CEO Robert Rabinovitch in a dispute over future hiring practices. The impact of the lockout rocked the nation. Television and radio programming ceased except for the airing of TV re-runs and BBC news. For anyone who worked in the central business district of any Canadian capital city, this meant seriously considering re-routing the walk to work so as to avoid the angry mob of CBC employees manning the picket lines who looked ready to throw tomatoes at any passersby who looked like management.

To describe CBC employees as enraged was an understatement. You see, there's a significant psychological difference between a strike and a lockout. In a strike, employees have control. They feel empowered and passionate about the cause. In a lockout situation, employees are literally locked out of their place of work, treated like trespassers, some even escorted out by security. The CBC crew were so pissed off they'd even started producing their own underground podcasts to make sure the public knew their truth.

It was late on a Wednesday afternoon in early September 2005 when Sylvie received the call. CBC had summoned a representative from the firm she was working with to come up with a strategy to help deal with the fallout expected from the lockout. They'd given her 48 hours to come up with a pitch. Given the notoriety of this situation, she knew that this gig could be a poisoned chalice and that if she failed her career was dust.

Sylvie told us that she wasn't sure whether it was God on her side, delusions of grandeur or fool's courage that was with her that morning. Maybe the fact that she had once trained as a journalist had given her an in with the executive. Whatever the reason, they trusted her within minutes. By the

---

6   Bryant, A. "Four Executives On Succeeding in Business as a Woman." *The New York Times* (2014), 12/10.

end of the meeting she had figured out a way to manage their workforce's return to work and deal with any emotional storms. As she recounts the day of her contract-winning pitch, she told us how surreal it still feels for her. How she managed to land one of the highest profile and politically charged jobs in Canadian union history still blows her mind.

The project was a roaring success. In just three weeks Sylvie and her team had rolled out the initiative in every major Canadian capital city. It was such a hit that their work even made the headlines a couple of times going from "How to heal a bruised workplace: CBC hires consultant to soothe nerves" to "Inspiration and renewal on the picket line." Fortuitously, this was just in time for the return to normal operations in mid-October and the commencement of Canada's most important television show, Hockey Night in Canada. Given Canada's obsession with the sport, our colleague told us that she couldn't help thinking that getting this program back on the air probably acted as an additional incentive to resolve the dispute.

Whatever it was, she was happy it was over. The experience working with the CBC executive and its 600 managers had been the most challenging and exhilarating experience of her professional career. It had been worth the fifteen-hour days, the four weeks she had spent living out of a suitcase, and the countless conversations consoling the plagued consciences of many of the executive who had not been thrown out on the street.

But the lockout was not without its consequences. The months of dispute and pressure had forever changed many of the executive team who struggled with survivor guilt and, despite all the coaching support, one of the female executives had even taken her own life. This was a bitter-sweet victory for CBC despite the fact that things had finally returned to normal.

It had been a gruelling assignment psychologically despite the satisfaction of a job well done, and Sylvie wondered what it would be like back at the office. Would she be treated like an Olympian, being welcomed back on home soil after winning the gold? The organisation was about to conduct annual performance reviews, and even though it had a reputation for being notoriously cheap and an old boys' club, she believed, like Kathryn, that her work with CBC could not be ignored and that at the very least, a raise in pay was imminent.

Sylvie met her boss at a hotel bar. He ordered them whiskies and got down to business. He gave her a few pats on the back and assured her he had big plans for her future. "It is so good that you are a career woman," he told her. "You're not like the others who keep going off and having children. You are a valuable asset for our company."

And then she got the real story about CBC.

"We want to congratulate you on the great job you did with CBC. To be honest we asked you to do the pitch because we thought you were the only one crazy enough to go in there and do it. We didn't expect you to win it."

Kick in the guts.

Sylvie's reward for a job so well done was a microscopic pay raise for reasons of inflation, and the promise of greatness in years to come, if, of course, she didn't go off and get pregnant. Oh, and the whiskey was on him too.

The Recognition Game

We've seen variations of Sylvie's story happen time and time again, at various level of an organisation, from the administrative assistant to the flashy vice president. It goes like this: person A does a tremendous job and goes the extra mile. Amidst much turbulence and roadblocks, she surpasses her targets and succeeds. Hooray!

Then what happens? She waits and hopes that someone, somewhere, is going to step up and acknowledge her success and reward the hell out of it.

But of course not much happens. We all have been there before and can relate to Sylvie: the answers from the Powers That Be are disappointing. We feel used or taken for granted.

Of course one can always protest and ask for more, but at that point, it is too little too late. Nobody wants to look like a whiner.

There are lessons to be learned from this.

Waiting for somebody's approval is a terrible position to be in. Counting on people to spot your talent and give you a pass upward is, more often than not, useless. The alternative is to try to take the matter into your own hands. Negotiate prior to engaging into a dare-devil task. Set your boundaries and own your agenda. Chances are that people will respect you for it.

Women are Worse Leaders than Men

The sad reality is that the behaviour of the executive leader in Sylvie's story is nothing new. There really does exist a deep-rooted belief that women are less effective leaders than men. In more traditional cultures like at our colleague's organisation at the time, this belief is an even greater contributing factor to the gender gap in leadership.

Women who are viewed as ambitious are also more likely to be penalised for their success[7]. Asking for recognition for a job well done, our colleague

---

7   Heilman, M.E., Wallen, A.S., Fuchs, D., Tamkins, M.M. "Penalties for Success: Reactions to Women Who Succeed at Male Gender-Typed Tasks." *Journal of Applied Psychology*, (2004), 89, 416-427.

was viewed as inappropriately demanding and aggressive. We know because we ended up doing a stint with the very same company and that's how they described her to me.

Kathryn Underwood, the protagonist of our case study, was even more vulnerable to gender bias. She was competing for the CEO's job in a culture with no history of female role models at the top. Research shows that men's perceptions are more likely to have an effect on female career outcomes in male-dominated domains like corporate leadership[8]. The playing field was not even close to being even, right from the start.

Kathryn didn't get the job of top dog at Kudos, but her story is a great example of a competent leader who displayed strong professional identity and authenticity without losing herself in the process. Kathryn Underwood "Leaned In,[9]" courageously pursuing her career goals with passion, confidence and fearlessness against all odds. Her example encourages us to strive harder and ask for more.

The Lesser-Known Threat

Kathryn's story also exposes a lesser-known threat that is perhaps even more dangerous to women reaching for their professional goals. We're talking about women that hold other women back. At Kudos, a traditional corporate culture, the lack of female representation at the top and the mentality of other women like Emma Darling and Mrs. White are commonplace obstacles for women wanting to get ahead.

As professional coaches, we like to keep the faith. We'd like to believe that this attitude is slowly changing through the examples of powerful women and organisations created to provide support for women leaders popping up around the globe[10]. High-profile leaders like Sheryl Sandberg and actors with clout like Emma Watson (of the Harry Potter franchise) are pioneers of our time. They utilize their fame and fortune to raise awareness of the need for women to help other women reach new professional heights and rectify the imbalance. They are trying making a difference.

To finish Sylvie's story: She is no victim. She describes herself as being one of the lucky ones to have been supported and celebrated by many inspiring and powerful women over the years.

---

8   Prime, J.L., Carter, N.M., Welbourne, T.M. "Women 'Take Care,' Men 'Take Charge': Managers' Stereotypic Perceptions of Women And Men Leaders. *The Psychologist-Manager Journal* (2009), 12, 25-49.

9   Sandberg, S. *Lean In: Women, Work and the Will to Lead.* Random House: UK, 2013.

10   Sarah Dinolfo, Christine Silva, and Nancy. M. Carter, *High Potentials in the Leadership Pipeline: Leaders Pay It Forward.* Catalyst, 2012, 7, 534-542.

A managing director from one of Canada's foremost human capital companies heard of her work on the CBC gig and gave her a call to find out more. She wanted to know who had won the contract out from her own prestigious organisation that had an elite reputation, and impressive portfolio of high profile clients.

Two months later Sylvie was looking out the window of her new office in Ottawa, marvelling at the view of the snow-dusted parliament buildings and planning the future of her new charge as "leader of the opposition."

We are often asked by our female clients to describe the characteristics that enable successful women to part the Red Sea and move into the upper echelons of power. There's no easy answer to that question, but here's what we tell our clients when they ask what it is going to take. In those women that persevere and make it, we have noticed they display the following pivotal characteristics: roaring courage, unshakeable confidence, a strong sense of justice, a burning desire be the master of their own destinies, and the belief that magic does happen.

Chapter 18 – It's All About Sex

Believe it or not, Kathryn's story sheds light on a phenomenon that is old news. We know that women crap on other women in the workplace in often vile and unforgivable ways, yet it is usually swept under the carpet and dismissed. Some would say it's just women being women. But why is it that some women can be so nasty? What is it that propels the Mrs. White's and Emma Darlings of this world to behave so badly? The answers might be found in Darwin's theory of evolution. We spoke to Andrew O'Keefe, author of Hardwired Humans: Successful Leadership Using Human Instincts[11], to provide a new perspective from the animal kingdom. He shed some light on the issues with us through the research he's been doing with Dr. Jane Goodall on chimps in captivity.

During mating season at Taronga Zoo in Sydney, Australia the primates are randy as hell and the female chimpanzees jostle to get as much action as possible. One of the chimps, Sally, got pregnant while another chimp, Josie, did not. Sally had her baby and Josie was so distraught over her inability to conceive that she turned her anger on Sally's infant and tried to kill it. She did not succeed. Several months later Josie conceived and had a baby. But Sally carried the memory of what Josie tried to do to Sally's baby. In a violent act of retribution, Sally killed Josie's baby.

This true story of vengeful female chimp behaviour is a poignant example of the lengths female primates take to hurt and punish other females in their community who have wronged them. Apparently, it's worse at the time of oestrus, the primate menstrual cycle, when female chimp aggression forces even the most magnanimous of alpha males to duck for cover.

O'Keefe's book provides us with an interesting analysis of the primate world to explain homo sapiens' workplace antics and demystify human behaviours. It leaves one to wonder if being bitchy is part of our DNA, or, are women behaving badly towards other women because of a conscious choice they make?

This may be a clear explanation as to why women fight dirty: it is rooted in primal animal behaviour. But why compare us to chimps? O'Keefe explains that it makes sense to draw comparisons because chimps are the socio-species closest to humans.

Just like in the workplace, the primate world has a hierarchical structure that provides the framework for social standing. Even among chimps, fe-

---

11   O'Keefe, A. *Hardwired Humans – Successful Leadership Using Human Instincts.* Roundtable Press: Australia, 2011.

male primates higher on the totem pole will often bully and socially ostracise females of lower ranking. So how can lower-level female chimps rise up in the primate ranks? It appears that genitals make the difference. The more engorged and swollen a female's genitals, the more attractive they become to the male chimps. So much so that chimps with the enhanced assets that were once bullied by the other females become coveted by the males in the tribe and protected against harm. It really is all about sex.

In our modern-day workplaces, where women are underrepresented at the upper echelons of power, we could expect the female primal instincts will kick in. Women would be more likely to engage in hyper-competitive behaviours in the face of scarce resources. Perhaps we're really not that different from our fellow chimps. In the animal world it's about procreation and survival. In our human world it's about getting ahead.

Not a lot of research exists on intra-sexual competition between females, but what we have discovered provides some interesting food for thought. In the quest for finding a mate, two competitive strategies that are most typically used by women are self-promotion and what's called derogation of rivals[12]. Self-promotion involves women trying to make themselves more attractive by wearing make-up and tight-fitting clothes. Derogation of rivals is about using indirect aggression to reduce the perceived mate value of a rival. Most common tactics include spreading rumours about the rival's fidelity and/or promiscuity, disparaging her appearance, excluding her from her peer group, or giving her the dreaded silent treatment.

As you can see, even if we're not talking about sex or the search for love, tactics some women use to bully other women are universal. That's why movies like Mean Girls have risen in popularity over recent years: they represent something very real happening in our everyday experience that has a massive impact on the way women learn to manage these situations later in life. And for the most part, they are not managed well.

Was Emma Darling justified in doing to Kathryn what came naturally? She spread rumours to destroy her reputation in order to increase her value in the eyes of her prospective mate, Preston Steele, and gain his favour. Did Emma have a choice in how she behaved, or were her natural instincts just far too strong?

Interestingly, the addition of female physical attractiveness adds another layer of complexity to the bitch fight phenomenon. Researchers have proven that women who are perceived as good looking are also more likely to

---

12 Vaillancourt, T., & Sharma, A. "Intolerance of Sexy Peers: Intrasexual Competition Among Women." *Aggressive Behaviour* (2011), 37, 569-577.

be punished by other women. This is because in the workplace, sex is often used as a weapon to get ahead or a driver to quash another.

Social scientists Baumeister and Twenge provide an explanation for this. They talk about a double standard of sexual morality that exists in which women "stifle each other's sexuality because sex is a limited resource that women use to negotiate with men, and scarcity gives women an advantage[13]." So here we are again back to basic primitive brain antics.

In a very illuminating Canadian study, psychologists Vallaincourt and Sharma put this belief to the test. They manipulated participant perceptions to test whether women behaved more nastily toward a sexily dressed woman versus a conservative-looking lady.

The result: all participants laughed, ridiculed and rolled their eyes at the sexily dressed woman, while in contrast there was no reaction at all to the conservatively dressed woman. This finding is consistent with evidence that women are threatened by, disapprove of, and punish women who appear too sexy by means of indirect aggression. What's more, women reported being less likely to be friends with the sexy woman, as the perceived perception for them to potentially steal their man is high.

How does all this play out in the workplace for women? Does adding a bit of sexiness to the mix assist or stifle a woman's career progression? To answer this question, let's turn to the world stage for real life examples.

In 2012, Melissa Nelson, a 33-year old dental assistant from Iowa, was fired by her boss, James Knight (after working for him for 10 years) for being too attractive. The court ruled that Knight acted legally in firing Nelson because he and his wife viewed her as a threat to their marriage. The court ruled 7–0 that bosses can fire employees they see as an irresistible attraction, even if they have not engaged in flirtatious behavior or otherwise done anything wrong.

In a follow-up interview Nelson also shared that her boss had considered her a stellar worker, but in the final months of her employment, he complained that her tight clothing was distracting, once telling her that if his pants were bulging that was a sign her clothes were too revealing.

Then there was Debrahlee Lorenzana. She lost her job at Citibank because her good looks made her co-workers feel uncomfortable.

These examples demonstrate the quandary good-looking women are placed in from both sexes. Being attractive will often help you get in the door, but it might not help to keep your job.

---

13   Baumeister, R. F., & Twenge, J. M. "Cultural Suppression of Female Sexuality." *Review General Psychology* (2002), 6, 166-203.

At the end of the day, it is time for women to take control over the way they behave. Whether you like or dislike another woman or not, doesn't warrant the cattiness and cruel treatment so often served up.

It's time to shift the pendulum on these behaviours and fight a natural urge to be mean. Part of the answer lies in becoming more aware. Bringing our unconscious instincts to a raised level of consciousness may be the answer to women being better able to manage their biases toward other women and halt the Jekyll and Hyde transformation.

The Best Friend Double Cross

We often receive calls for help from women suffering from one of the most devastating psychological work-related injuries: being double crossed by their best friend at work.

The situation is inevitably explained to us with this narrative: "I had a best friend at work and we had bonded over a common goal (getting through, overcoming a bad boss, succeeding, etc.). We confided in each other, shared our aspirations, dreams and struggles – the whole nine yards! Then one day something shifted. Maybe it's because we were getting too close. I couldn't help measuring myself against her and vice-versa. When it was time for a promotion, we wished each other good luck and hugged. But it was all phony and I later learned that she got the job by talking behind my back. In hindsight, the green-eyed monster had taken over and reason walked out the door taking our years of friendship with it."

The above, or a variation of this scenario, is what we hear all the time. It's a well-known fact that should not be forgotten: closeness with someone from the same sex brings comparison, which breeds envy, jealousy and, ultimately, the drive to act on those feelings. It's the shadow side of human interactions and while we sometimes like to think all is rosy and pure, that shadow very much exists and is a force to be reckoned with.

For some women, it goes back a long way, all the way down to their original rivalries with their siblings. Perhaps it was a big sister that brought you down, or the family's baby girl who used her youthful charm to undermine you every time she got a chance. That's what we are talking about. And what were you fighting about anyway? Psychoanalysis taught us it was about the Oedipus complex and that yes, it's all about sex.

Chapter 19 – Word from the Street

Bitchy women in the workplace who play emotional and tormenting games are also responsible for high levels of stress and sickness among their female colleagues. It is also one of the foremost blockers to female career progression. So just how prevalent is women-on-women bullying in the workplace? While it's difficult to pin down a number with precision, some stats are worth noting. Indeed, recent research usually points out that anywhere from 46% to 52% of women say that they have experienced workplace bullying or harassment over the preceding three years, more than half of it by another woman. In other words, while it is considered that 60% of bullies are men, women are still more likely to be bullied by another woman. All in all, it is estimated that around 30% of workplace bullying is women-on-women. To top if off, the occurrence seems to be on the way up[14].

Given the high frequency of women bullying other women in the workplace, you might assume that reams of research exist providing a bulletproof roadmap to help those going through the experience to navigate the situation and not become a victim of its aftermath. In reality very little published information exists on this topic, part of the reason why we were so spurred on to share Kathryn's story.

To gather more meaningful data, we hit the streets to seek out real-life stories from women in Australia, Canada, and Bali who were willing to share their struggles with members of the same-sex.

What really hit home for us was how difficult it was for women who had been part of a bitch fight to move on from the experience. The devastation caused by the bullying was still palpable. There were also those who had been energised by the experience and had, like Kathryn, come back triumphant, but they were fewer than the former.

So why aren't women going public with this? Why isn't a very real threat to female health and wellbeing getting discussed?

It's because it's taboo – and on a couple of levels.

Firstly, women who out their sisters are seen by other women as disloyal traitors.

To illustrate, take Meredith Fuller, a psychologist for 30 years and author of the book Working with Bitches: Identify the Eight Types of Office Mean

---

14 From the workplace bullying institute: http://www.workplacebullying.org/wow-bullying/.

Girls and Rise Above Workplace Nastiness[15]. Dr. Fuller's book sparked an outrage amongst female critics and a spate of vicious attacks as she was seen as deepening the great divide of male and female inequality by not supporting her sisters in the writing of her book.

On the contrary, after so many years of working with clients who commonly complained against the school-yard style bullying and exclusion tactics women use to get their own way at work, Dr. Fuller's work provides compelling evidence to suggest how women get in their own way. Her book forces us to evaluate our own level of inner bitch to become more consciously aware and defend against gender bias rather than being part of the problem.

Secondly, what makes bitch fight antics difficult to discuss is that women who are seen to protest or confront the bitches, risk being perceived as petty, overemotional or high maintenance by others in the workplace. Research demonstrates that women who have had interpersonal difficulties with a female co-worker are viewed more negatively than men and will most likely be overlooked for future career opportunities. Moreover, women involved in female/female conflict hold grudges and are less likely to work productively in the future.

Case in point: We'll always remember our client Monica. Just six months after she was ambushed by a female peer and unjustifiably lost the trust of many of her colleagues, Monica was still reeling. She did not fight back or quit her job even though her working situation had become unbearable. She went silent. Every day at work was like Groundhog Day, going through the motions in a zombie-like state just to get to 5 o'clock. She figured it was better to hide than to create waves and get punished for it. She had mentally checked out.

Interestingly enough, what eventually kicked her out of her slump was the realisation that she was getting a dose of some serious karma. You see, Monica was also guilty of mistreating other women. It wasn't until the shoe was on the other foot that she had realised the full impact of her actions.

"Being honest about how guilty I felt about being a bitch is a place we all need to go if we are to change," she told us.

For Monica it was not until she was on the receiving end of a bitch fight that she was able to take stock off her own inner biases toward other women. Light switch on.

---

15   Fuller, M. *Working with Bitches: Identify the Eight Types of Office Mean Girls and Rise Above Workplace Nastiness*. Dacapo Press, 2013.

Moving on from a Bully's Attack

You can help a woman who has been on the receiving end of a female bully move on with her life. While there are no perfect recipes for a successful intervention, there are a few pointers worth underlining.

The first order of business is to listen and try to understand. This can take a while. A certain amount of trust has to be established before one feels comfortable opening up. Stories get mixed up, hesitations creep in, there's excessive minimisation and even feelings of guilt. There can also be sudden bursts of self-blame: "I'm probably overreacting," "It's not that bad," "I'm too emotional," Don't worry!" It is important to be patient and respect the person's rhythm and various defence mechanisms. We wish it all worked out easily. There are a number of potential pitfalls along the way.

To illustrate, when we saw Kathryn, months after her ordeal, she was living as a recluse and was shattered. At first she simply needed to vent and we were her sounding board, often staying quiet. Our efforts to help her were met with moderate success, but this was a necessary step. She tried, but was unable to really articulate what had happened to her. She struggled to make sense of her experience. The psychological blockers that stunted her path to recovery were self-blame and anger. She blamed herself for everything that had gone wrong. She felt like a failure. She was angry with herself for not reading the play better, for allowing herself to be bullied. She was angry with everyone else for their subterfuge, for the emotional abuse, for the lack of support and belief in her.

Working with Kathryn, it was obvious that there was not one person that had been the catalyst for her sadness. What stood out was her deep resentment toward Mrs. White and the treatment she'd endured at her hands during her time at Kudos.

Kathryn needed to take the time to talk through her emotions and work things out in her mind. While Kathryn talked, our role evolved and we became more like jazz musicians. We improvised on the themes and moods that emerged, alternating from quiet listening, reconstruction, re-formulation, pushing back, re-focusing etc., all with the goal of having her take stock of what had happened. She needed a fresh perspective to be able to take greater control of her next steps.

We weren't able to sort out every last detail of her story, as there was plenty we couldn't figure out: Mrs. White's motives, the responsibility she had in some events, why she could not help repeat some old patterns, to name a few. However, that was not the point. The point was not to reach the absolute truth and figure out everything. The objective was for her to have enough clarity to move on.

One of the most difficult things to do in life is to move on from unfinished business without closure. Yet sometimes, for our own sanity, we just have to get on with life without closure. Kathryn needed to move on from this experience. She needed to turn her back on the past to move forward.

We recall a client's story about a visit to a Buddhist Monastery in Thailand. The client was trying to recover from a bitter divorce and jump back into life with a more positive attitude. He recounted the story the monks shared with him that really helped to jolt him out of a slump.

"You need to imagine yourself standing at a doorway with a big, heavy suitcase. The threshold of the doorway represents your current life. The suitcase represents your past. In order to move into the future, you must drop that suitcase behind you, walk through the door and slam it shut. Leave the past in the past. Don't let your past become an anchor around your neck. Move forward into the sun, into your future, and don't look back or try to open the door again."

We asked Kathryn to stand up, pass through the threshold of her present and walk into the future of the life she wanted.

The Victim Trap

With Kathryn, it went pretty well overall and we were able to get her back in shape in decent time. Sometimes it does not work out so well and it is important to explain why that may be.

To sum it up succinctly: don't fall into the victim trap, i.e. don't dwell for too long on variations of "I was screwed!" or "This bitch had it in for me!" or "I'm the victim here!"

Excessive victimisation is a treacherous path to take and must be avoided at all costs. However, it's a very tricky deal because (as we know from Kathryn story) acknowledging what happened and not feeling guilty about it is part of the recovery process. In others words, partially accepting being put in the victim seat is part of the path to feeling better. The risk is in getting stuck on it forever.

The same principles hold true for those who include in their recovery process the act of naming what they went through, be it psychological harassment, bullying, emotional abuse, etc.

Being able to articulate and name your truth is a crucial part of the legitimising and healing process. The danger is the label becomes a psychological handcuff. By handcuff, we mean that you define yourself only by that label. To truly move on also means breaking away from these shackles.

Working through this with a trained mental healthcare professional is advisable. It makes sense to start by inquiring about services your company has to offer to support employees going through tough times. Before sharing, ensure that you don't tell your stories from a purely emotional angle. You need to have sufficient facts gathered and be able to share them calmly without sounding dramatic and overly emotional.

Most organisations are usually ill-prepared to deal with bullying and may tend to water down any given conflict and/or see it as a personality clash where both sides are to blame. If you've been taken down hard, you don't need a mediator, you need the law to be on your side. Bottom line: if you feel too banged up and uncertain, it may be better to ask for external help first, if only to help you sort things out.

CHAPTER 20 – STANDING UP TO THE FEMALE BULLY

In writing this book we anticipated a backlash from female colleagues, friends and strangers. We were getting ready to dodge a barrage of rotten tomatoes much like Dr. Meredith Fuller for her book, Working with Bitches. To road test the content of Bitch Fight we accepted an invitation from a national Australian association for women to give a free talk on the subject to their members. We were expecting the worst. Many women we had previously discussed our book's subject matter with had been appalled that we had even written it.

"How dare you stigmatise women as being bitchy!" some said, while others were of the opinion that our book would "only fuel those women-haters out there!"

Others took offence at our use of the term bitch, arguing that it had a natural negative connotation and only served to highlight "women's inhumanity to other women[16]."

But these women were in a minority.

We walked into a sold out auditorium of almost 100 women who were highly engaged by what we had to say. There was no anger, no defensiveness, and not a tomato in sight. Instead, something amazing happened. Many of the participants bonded over this topic that had left many of them with very real pain and anxiety during the course of their careers. Individuals stood up in succession to share their stories and seek coaching and support from the others in the group to help work through the bitch fight scenarios they had to manage. The healing in the room was palpable. This was the closest we had seen to what a real, true women's club might look like, and what it would feel like to be part of; it was powerful.

What came from the group was a crucial need to understand how female-on-female bitch fighting equates to a lesser-known, yet insidious form of bullying. Insidious because it is so often invisible to others.

The Worst Kind of Psychological Bullying

Most people have a pretty sound intuitive idea of what bullying is and of what kind of behaviours are used to express it. However, we found there remains a significant number of ambiguities and myths involved in its comprehension and it is thus worth providing some clarification.

It is worth underlining again: what we are describing in this book is a phenomenon that goes way beyond women snubbing or being cold towards

---

16   Chesler, P. *Woman's Inhumanity to Woman*. New York: Nation Book, 2002.

one another. We are talking about the worst kind of bullying that is defined as "a destructive process consisting of a succession of hostile statements and action which, if taken in isolation, may seem more or less harmless, but whose constant repetition have pernicious and devastating effects[17]" unleashed by women onto other women. Real, legitimate bullying is not a one-time occurrence. It is a pattern of behaviours and/or a series of incidents that takes place frequently and over time.

These bullying tactics are "repeated verbal or psychological attacks or intimidations that are intended to cause fear, distress or harm to the victim[18]."

Note the word intend. If this were a criminal trial, all the prosecution would have to prove to have someone incarcerated is they have displayed mens rea (an intent to kill), not whether or not they had actually succeeded. You can see where we are going with this.

Psychological bullying behaviours are considered forms of direct (obvious) and indirect (subtle) aggression. Tactics range from intimidation, verbal threats, and constant criticism, to deliberately undermining a person's work, setting someone up to fail, and spreading rumours, to name a few. Bullying can also be about committing acts of commission (doing things to others) or omission (withholding resources from others)[19].

What distinguishes bullying in the workplace from the regular garden variety described above? The description in the literature describes characteristic phases that build up over time to maximise its impact. Here's one example of how a female on female bullying scenario may build up over time:

Victims of bullies are first exposed to frequent fault-finding and criticism. At the same time, victims report repeated attempts to undermine their position, status, worth, value and/or potential[20]. This psychological battering is likely to cause a feeling of isolation. Typically, individuals may then withdraw and disengage from work in order to manage the psychological issues that are beginning to appear. The victim's self-confidence is taken a beating.

The second phase of workplace bullying begins when the victim is clearly singled out and treated differently from others. Constantly under the microscope, they cannot get away with anything. Worst yet, their responsi-

17   Leymann, H. "The Content and Development of Mobbing at Work." *European Journal of Work and Organizational Psychology* (1996). 5, 165-184.

18   Farrington, D.P. "Understanding and Preventing Bullying." *Crime and Justice* (1993), (17) 381-458. The University of Chicago Press: Chicago.

19   From http://www.workplacebullying.org/individuals/impact/mental-health-harm/.

20   Namie, G. & Namie, Ruth. "U.S. Workplace bullying: Some Basic Considerations and Consultation Interventions." *Consulting Psychology Journal: Practice and Research*, (2009), 61(3), 202-219.

bilities increase but their area of control or influence shrinks as they are squeezed from all size and corners. At this stage, the decline in performance becomes obvious and the victim can no longer cope with the unrealistic demands of the job. The victim is beginning to crumble.

In the final phase, the victim finds that everything they say is twisted around and misrepresented. The trap has been laid out and they have no more room to manoeuvre. The bully is in control, waiting for the final blow to eliminate the victim once and for all. It's game over!

You can see how important it is to be able to recognise the early warning signs of bullying. Being prepared to take action before you're too caught up in the web that's been spun is key to remaining buoyant and outsmarting the bully before your self-esteem is in tatters and you have no energy left to fight.

Rise of the Queen Bee

At a fundamental level, this high incidence of gender and status inequality has not surprisingly created fertile soil for the emergence of women known as queen bees. Queen bees are typically personified by ambitious women wanting to maintain their power in their jobs and get ahead. One has to only turn to characters like Miranda in the Hollywood blockbuster Devil Wears Prada and Alexis Colby in Dynasty to see stereotypical female bullies in action. These are women who have succeeded but who refuse to help other women do the same.

More specifically, the "Queen Bee Syndrome" is a phenomenon defined in the early seventies for highly successful women who have reached the top of their game who are regarded as even more sexist and ruthless that their male counterparts. Queen bees will usually distance themselves from other females who they perceive as competition, refuse to assist them and block their rise up the ranks.

Our Mrs. White is a great live example of a queen bee in action. She was committed to blocking Kathryn's success in the role despite her being the better candidate. Mrs. White perceived Kathryn's presence at the executive table as a social threat diminishing her own power and status.

Finally, in the world of business where female role models at the top are barely there and higher positions for women in leadership remain more elusive than commonplace, female war tactics are on the rise. One only has to look to the media to be overwhelmed a daily inundation of stories of workplace bullying, gender discrimination, and tragic accounts of people taking their own lives because of their inability to fight back against abusive behaviour experienced at work.

At the end of the day what is clear is that instead of women supporting one another at work, a dog-eat-dog situation is occurring where only the toughest survive. Yes, it's the office bitches that get ahead and, yes it is usually the bully that gets promoted. There's a reason why the phrase "nice girls finish last" was coined: because it's often true. However, in the grand scheme of things, there are no real winners – only survivors waiting for the next round of fighting.

Scientists argue that perhaps what perpetuates this behaviour lies in the degree to which a workplace culture or industry is male-dominated and sexist. In other words, a male dominated environment may naturally incite female-on-female bitch fighting. Why? Well, we live in turbulent times of economic uncertainty and despite our sophisticated appearance, women are still human animals competing for scarce resources and feeling under threat.

It seems that the world of work has become an arena where only the fittest survive.

Chapter 21- Enter the Psychopath

Data shows that around 4% of corporate professionals can safely be described as having psychopathic tendencies. To give it another spin, one out of every 25 leaders passing through any given company is not the kind of individual someone wants as his boss. When you view this through a ten to fifteen-year lens and, knowing the dawdling rate at which some companies move out their executives, the number suddenly becomes quite significant.

According to the Workplace Bullying Institute, when you add bullying to the mix, up to one third of workers may be the victims of workplace bullying. Generally speaking, it is assumed about 40% of workplace bullies are women, an alarming figure for such an underplayed and underrepresented phenomenon. Compared to males, it is found that female bullies are way more likely to bully other females. Males, on the other hand, are considered equal-opportunity offenders as they bully males and females equally.

One can't help but wonder what type of person is capable of bullying someone else. The million-dollar question for us in writing this book was, can anyone be a bully? The short answer is that it does take a specific psychological makeup to be a serial bullying offender. As human beings we are all capable of being mean on occasion. To repeatedly plot, scheme and intend to psychologically destroy someone else is an entirely different ballgame. It is critical to be able to distinguish between the two.

The psychopath is a person who manifests an amoral and antisocial behaviour. They have extreme egocentricity, a lack of or little ability to love or show empathy, or establish meaningful personal relationships[21].

There's no need to be an expert to grasp the type of behaviours a psychopath exhibits or understand the havoc they create in the lives of the people they touch. We are surrounded by more psychopaths than one realizes. Take a look at your daily newspapers and you'll be bombarded by descriptions of morally deprived individuals of all sorts: cold-blooded killers, predators and other emotionless nut jobs.

Are the psychopaths at work just as bad? In reality, only a small number of psychopaths commit the heinous crimes we so often witness on the 6 o'clock news. The more pedestrian psychopath is not usually overly violent, anti-social or as dramatic as what we read about[22]. While they do thrive on

---

21 Babiak, P. & Hare, R. D. *Snakes in Suits: When Psychopaths Go to Work*. New-York: Harper-Collins, 2006.

22 Kets de Vries, M. F. R. "The Psychopath in the C Suite: Redefining the SOB." Working paper (2012) – more info at http://www.ketsdevries.com/author/papers/.

delusions of world domination and are compelled to abuse and humiliate others at every turn, they do not usually engage in lawless behaviours.

Bitch-fighting bullies at work sit at the lower end of the psychopathic spectrum. They are no Jeffrey Dahmer. In practical terms this means they do not readily engage in externalised violent acts. They are instead master chameleons, usually with polished outward appearances and carefully managed stage effects. So much so that they blend in to organisational life quite well and go undiscovered for a long time.

Other characteristics that are used to describe the psychopathic executives are narcissistic, exploitative, charming on the surface but domineering at the core, Machiavellian, conniving, risk-takers, thriving on chaos, masters at bending the truth and using it to their advantage, and masterful political animals.

How Far Would You Go?

We are all capable of being a bully to some degree without having a full-fledged personality disorder. Competitive, performance driven and/or cut-throat environments where the law of the jungle reigns supreme naturally tends to bring out uglier behaviours in just about everybody. Specific contexts, cultures and/or authority figures can also be powerful influencers. Think back to the famous Milgram experiment from 1963.

Stanley Milgram was a psychologist at Yale University, who conducted an experiment in understanding how far people would go in obeying an instruction if it involved harming another person. To do this he wanted to see if people could be convinced to give punishment (electric shock) to other individuals if instructed to do so by someone they perceived as an authority figure. The results were shocking.

Most of the participants under direct instruction administered up to 450 volts of electricity to those who gave the wrong answers. Milgram's experiment demonstrated how ordinary people would follow orders given by an authority figure, especially those they recognised as morally right or based on a legal rationale. They were also prepared to punish perceived offenders if the authority figure promised to take the blame for the punishment they would inflict on others. Milgram held that the reactions he witnessed were ingrained in people from their upbringing, which they then brought into the workplace. Milgram's experiment serves as a startling reminder of how even good people with the best of intentions can be convinced to perform acts conflicting with their personal conscience and inflict harm on others.

There are many differences between regular people and psychopaths. At a low-end level, part of it is purely self-control. When it's all said and done, bitch fighting is at its very core still about exercising power and domination, usually with career advancement in mind. In a dog-eat-dog world, where competition is at the fore and only the tough survive, all of us are tested daily.

In situations of domestic violence and other forms of abuse, it is a well-known fact that victims will frequently become the perpetrators of the very act that caused them so much pain. We will never forget a very successful senior executive of an IT organisation we worked with who was known to crap on other women. She justified her behaviour with this: "I did what I had to do. Don't blame the player, blame the game."

How Do You Spot a Psychopath at Work?

The incidence of workplace psychopathology, particularly in successful leaders is a frequent occurrence. Much like the essence of our discussion in this book about women mistreating other women, it is a phenomenon that is commonplace, yet not discussed.

For Kathryn there were more than a few adversaries blocking the yellow brick road to her Oz who manifested potential psychopathological characteristics. The challenge for Kathryn was in being able to distinguish between those with real psychological disturbances, bullies on a power trip, and people simply behaving badly.

In our coaching work, we spend a lot of time helping clients like Kathryn know how to deal with snakes in suits successfully. One of the biggest issues in being able to identify them is acknowledging they are not in fact a figment of our imagination. Indeed, it is difficult for the saner mind to understand how it is that such individuals could stay above an organisation's radar for any length of time. Yet, the answer is simple – the psychopath is a social mastermind and will often fit perfectly in a setting where influence, money, and status are front and centre and where power games are part of the daily grind. They flourish in a context where political skills, rather than competence, are keys to the top[23].

Also referred to as the psychopathic executive, this specific animal will usually occupy top leadership positions in environments where many of their character traits – extreme competitiveness, coolness under pressure,

---

23   Kets de Vries, Manfred, F.R. "The Psycho-path to Disaster: Coping with SOB Executives." *Organisational Dynamics*, 2014, Volume 43, no 1, pp. 17-26.

domination, ruthless political aggression, etc. – which would otherwise be frowned upon, are freely tolerated and even celebrated.

The acclaimed documentary The Corporation (2003) poignantly exposed through various case studies how an organisation, considered a legal entity, came to adopt and promote psychopath-like destructive behaviours. We see through their example how psychopathology can permeate an organisation via the hiring, grooming and promoting of individuals with similar psychological makeup.

Preston Steele fit the psychopath shoes perfectly. Problem was, Kathryn did not see him coming nor did she recognise how dangerous he was. From our conversations with her, it seemed that she was like most naïve individuals – blinded by his charisma and good looks, which had produced a kind of halo effect. The halo effect is also known as the "physical attractiveness stereotype"[24] or the "what is beautiful is good" principle. Because Preston was charming and attractive, Kathryn naturally perceived him as a good person. She was not alone in this. The halo effect around Preston was widespread, enabling him to exploit all the weaknesses and stressors that plagued Kudos and use them to his advantage.

It is critical for people to be aware of the existence of psychopaths in the workplace and know how to manage them accordingly. There's strength in numbers. To overthrow these bullies, solidarity and mass support for staging a coup d'état is critical. Unfortunately, Kathryn was not educated enough about the modus operandi of the psychopath at work to be able to manage him successfully out of the business before she went for the top job.

Stakeholder Mapping 101

The world is full of slimy sociopaths like Preston Steele and social climbers like Emma Darling. It always amazes us how many of our clients refuse to acknowledge that jerks like these are just part of everyday working life and that learning to manage these characters is a must for anyone wanting to get ahead.

The first rule is to find out everything you can about them: who they are, what makes them tick, what their motivations are, who are they connected to. Then you establish a good relationship with them. Machiavelli gave us sage advice when he told us to stay close to our friends and even closer to our enemies. Kathryn didn't like Preston and kept her distance from him rather than forging a stronger connection. To be honest, this is a natural reaction for most of us. To really turn the situation around to our advantage

---

24   Standing, L. G., in The SAGE Encyclopedia of Social Science Research Methods, Volume 1, 2004.

we must do that which makes us most uncomfortable – be around people we don't like or respect.

Kathryn's candidacy for the CEO role was hurt because she couldn't predict what his approach would be or whose support he would have, and was unable to tug on his heartstrings for her own battle for the role given there was no emotional connection between them. This meant that Preston was singularly focussed on winning the race for the top job at all costs without a pinch of loyalty or care for how it affected Kathryn.

In our coaching work with Kathryn, long before the opportunity for the CEO's role came up, we advised her to begin to foster relationships with key stakeholders at Kudos, particularly those she had an aversion to that could significantly impact her career goals in the long term. We went through a process of stakeholder mapping to determine how best to communicate and build key relationships in the business and externally. We also worked with Kathryn to identify what level of nurture was required to increase the quality and connection of many of these pivotal relationships.

For Preston, we advised her to find his weakness or some way in which she could be of service to him to become invaluable. After all, Kathryn was highly skilled in ingratiating herself by being of assistance. Finding some way to give him something that no one else could to help him fulfil his motivations was a key strategy. Keeping her finger on Preston's pulse and staying close by would have meant she would have had more control over his impact.

Unfortunately, like many of our clients, Kathryn's dislike of Preston overrode her ability to keep him close. Imagine if she'd known how he'd gotten his job at Kudos. Imagine if she knew him so well that she could whisper in the ear of the selection panel and other executives at Kudos and sway their judgment of him more in line with the truth versus what he had projected. Imagine if she'd been able to predict his strategy for winning the role so that she could trump him with her own.

To be successful as a leader, we recommend keeping your friends close, and your enemies closer.

Being stabbed in the back and bullied is painful. It hurts us deeply because it harms, violates, damages, and confounds us at the deepest parts of ourselves.

We have been witness to countless clients going through the pain and torment of being bullied. Indeed, a large part of the inspiration for this book was a special woman we worked with who ended up taking her own life as a reaction to years of being bullied by another female executive on her team. Crystal, like many women at the executive table, believed she had to be tough as nails, act like a man, and not share her emotions in order to be taken seriously. She suffered in silence for years while her pride and self-respect took a beating to the point of no return. Like Kathryn, she had driven to her lake house for some welcome respite. The only difference was, she went for a midnight swim and never came back.

We will never forget some enlightening insights that the CEO of a food manufacturing company shared with us about life at the top. It helped us to really empathise with the pre-existing feelings of isolation of being a leader many of our male and female executives feel, even without the addition of a bullying experience.

He said, "You know, I can't really talk to anyone. When you get into this job if you share your weaknesses, fears, and emotions you are seen as incompetent and not fit to run the company. So obviously I can't talk to the Board about this. I can't talk to my peers because they are in competition with me and will use stuff I say to their advantage. I can't talk to my direct reports because they'll just lose respect for me and see me a useless leader who they wouldn't like to follow. That's why I hired you guys; you are my safe place."

Watching a beautiful soul like Crystal psychologically unravel was tantamount to watching a slow death. For Crystal, and many people who are bullied, it is the personalised nature of bullying that destabilizes and disassembles a person's identity and ego bit by bit. What follows are inordinate feelings of frustration, an overwhelming sense of injustice, helplessness and profound sadness for almost anyone who has gone through it.

This begs the question: why do people stay silent about this invisible epidemic? Why didn't Crystal ask for help or make a stand to fight against what was happening to her? We know it's because she rationalised it, blamed herself, made excuses. Like most type-A Wonder Woman sorts, she felt like she should be able to handle it and explain it away.

"I'm probably over-sensitive," she told us. "It's just a personality difference, a style issue, I'm taking things too personally."

It is normal to have mixed feelings, guilt for having given so much control to the bully, and then shame and humiliation for not having done enough to put an end to it. One thing is certain: the longer the exposure to the stressor, the more severe the psychological impact will be. Psychosomatic symptoms such as anxiety, panic attacks, depression and post-traumatic stress usually follow.

When it is all said and done, it is a sad reality that it takes a person feeling unwell and a trip to the doctor before the real impact of bullying is finally discovered. There is no point in going through a potential ordeal all alone. Get out of the arena before the attacks get worse, and save yourself. Sometimes, simply taking the time to put your ideas together and discuss it with a trusted advisor helps put things in perspective. Talking and sharing often helps. You are not alone and there is no shame in expressing honestly what you are experiencing. Plus, there are experts out there. Why not benefit from their experience?

One of our coaches shared an interesting client's perspective: "I spent months alone ruminating… struggling to decide if I was being a drama queen or if there was really something to be worried about. Months! After I shared my situation with my ex-mentor, he laid down the law and helped me figure out a game plan in a thirty-minute conversation. I felt like a fool – a relieved fool – but a fool nonetheless for having waited so long."

The Quiet Achiever Rarely Wins the Race

Women are socialised to play nice. From the time we're born we're forced into the mould of caregiver and nurturer to prepare us for our potential future roles as wives and mothers. Once we hit the working world it's no different. Most women continue to respect our traditionally ascribed roles, play by the social rules, and feel that being thought of as a bitch is akin to having rabies.

In this context, it is easy to see how the early signs of being abused and/or bullied can be minimised or tossed aside. Women are not ready for a fight. Worst yet, they tend to project on others this aura of niceness they have integrated. In other words, they expect others to be like them: nice and well meaning. When it turns out somebody is not, they are unprepared and caught off guard.

In our leadership story, Kathryn behaved as you would expect any good woman to behave before her move to become CEO of Kudos. She was accommodating and gracious. She often put others first at her own expense. Feeling needed and playing the sacrificial lamb made her feel good. It met her need to feel like a good person, a person that people would like.

There's no denying that her great interpersonal skills and natural way of engaging also helped forge a successful career at Kudos. Her political savvy didn't hurt her career either. Kathryn raised her political capital in the organisation by engaging in generous acts of service. She ingratiated herself by being nice, low maintenance and easy to get along with, and it was her caring, service-oriented style that won friends and helped her to influence people to get ahead.

However, the reality is what got Kathryn the vice president's role wouldn't get her into the CEO's chair. Kathryn was not viewed as the natural successor to the CEO despite her impressive track record and high likeability quotient.

This is because being nice and caring is not associated with strength. It is seen as weak and soft. Her tendency to be overly consultative in an effort to appear collaborative did not help her cause either. It just made her appear indecisive. As is the case for so many other women, we knew if Kathryn was to have any chance of making it to the top, she needed to shake off the Mary Poppins image and be seen as tougher, able to stand alone in her decision-making, and she needed to build a stronger base of allies both inside and outside Kudos to increase her personal brand and market value. To be seen as the future CEO of Kudos, Kathryn had to exude strength without being seen as aggressive or as trying to be one of the guys at work.

Women have a really hard time doing that. They are socialised to put everyone else first. So it boils down to yet another fight against instinct to survive.

Making the Shift from Nice Girl to Warrior

Making the change can be pretty simple. There exists a plethora of evidence to demonstrate that as effective as some leaders may be, success is not guaranteed as a result. This is where many effective leaders like Kathryn miss the mark. She made the assumption that the mere fact of doing a good job and her staff liking her warranted a promotion and more likely paved the way for a step up. Interestingly, this urban myth is rife in the corporate world where the notion of the quiet achiever eventually becoming a powerful leader provides an excuse for many, particularly the more introverted, to fly under the radar and hide in their cubicles. The result is usually that they remain where they have placed themselves, unknown and under a rock.

It is important to build your profile because the the organisational landscape is inherently a political arena. Traditional decision-making models based on hierarchy no longer account for the reality that organisational decisions don't usually reflect the principles of fairness, rationality and professionalism, but rather reflect the informal power struggles designed to protect or enhance the self-interest of conflicting individuals or groups. This creates opportunity for slime bags like Preston to be more successful at climbing the leadership ladder than Kathryn. Despite her impressive track record and great interpersonal skills, she had an unwillingness to jump into the political ring. Preston was a fierce competitor because he knew the stakes were high and was proactive about playing the game.

Countless men and women we have coached over the years have expressed their distaste for promoting themselves and getting noticed. There's no mistaking that Kathryn's reluctance to raise her profile, coupled with her lack of desire to convert any potential saboteurs into raving fans, meant that she shot herself in the foot. We were hoping it wasn't too late for her to step up.

It can be difficult to get someone to toughen up and become a warrior. Nobody wants to become someone they feel is not consistent with their true self. One way to mitigate this fear is to make a clear distinction between the work persona and the family/friend persona. In other words, you can shine up your warrior armour at work and keep being nice to your friends – one does not exclude the other.

The objective is to tap into strong personality traits or idiosyncrasies and then leverage them fully. One example is Suzie. She had the gift of gab and knew how to put forward powerful arguments. Unfortunately, she used to tone it down in fear of being overbearing. We coached her to instead raise the volume on her verbal strengths and strive to make them her main weapon at work. In time, she became known for her ability to stand her ground and call people's mean-spirited attacks right off the bat. She might not have become the ultimate warrior, but she knew enough to defend herself with what she had to give.

There's a lesson in here for anyone with powerful leadership aspirations who resists the urge to get noticed because they believe actions speak for themselves. It means it's probably time to jump into the discomfort and get on the radar. Proactive and graceful self-promotion is a sophisticated and essential leadership skill.

CHAPTER 23 – WELCOME TO THE JUNGLE

In a March 19, 2013 article on Mumbrella's advertising boss Ian Perrin, he lamented about the lack of women at the top and asked for someone, anyone, to tell him why it was so. "Given that I don't have the answers probably makes me part of the problem," Perrin said. "If male CEOs such as myself can't understand the cause of the issue then there is little chance of us being part of the solution. So I would love to know why."

It is a great question. What is the male view about women being under represented at the top, and are they even aware of the women-on-women bullying taking place in the workplace? Men must have at least been privy to some serious episodes of bitch fighting over the years. Right?

Based on the frequency of corrosive female antics and the lack of inci-dences reported, we could only come up with two explanations. Either men were utter cowards and were simply turning a blind eye to it, or, they didn't even know it was going on. Judging by Perrin's statement, we guessed it was probably the latter.

Albeit inconclusive, some interesting research supports that in general men have a tendency to underplay women-on-women bullying. Men also tend to have a broader interpretation of what constitutes non-bullying be-haviours, especially if the target is female[25]. Other research shows that men are more prone to consider harassment perpetrated by women as less serious or view the female victim as provocative, laying more blame on the target's own behaviour and choices.

To put our theories to the test we interviewed over 50 senior male lead-ers to get their perspective on what they think is really going on. Here's an overview of what we heard:

Yes, I've seen it happen. I have seen it happen many times. This is not based on anything scientific or anything like that but I do feel like women are less straightforward in their attack. It is more under-handed you know? They'll gossip somebody out of a job – that sort of thing. How do I feel about it? I don't encourage it but it is part of cor-porate life. If you are in a competitive setting you will get whacked, fairly or unfairly, straight to your face or behind your back. May the best survive! – *Edward F., Group COO, loyalty business.*

---

25   Salin, D. "Bullying and Organisational Politics in Competitive and Rapidly Changing Work Environments." *International Journal of Management and Decision Making*, 2003, 4 (1), 35-46.

For sure it happens! Cat fight! Cat fight! Now if it is a one-way assault and one party does not know what is happening ... well, it is not as entertaining. How do I feel about it? I don't feel anything. It does not concern me, I don't interfere. I fight my battles and let others deal with theirs. – *Patrick S., Senior VP Finance, banking industry.*

It exists for sure but it is not a big deal for me. I guess it is because I never went with the premise that women would bond together in the first place. You understand where I'm coming from? If you go in with the idea that women would generally tend to help out each other then I guess you could be taken aback when they don't. But I never thought that. I expect them to bond when it serves them and undermine each other when they have to – just like men! – *Robert F., VP Finance, retail industry.*

Listen, this place is a jungle. We all act nice but it is a jungle. So that's it. Everybody does what you describe. Women, men, young and old, it does not matter. Is it taboo? Not to me! If it was, I would not be here to discuss it with you! – *Mike T., VP Marketing, gaming industry.*

I would like to believe that this does not happen here. Maybe it does to some extent but it is no big deal, it is little petty things, some gossip sure. I think cream always rises to the top you know? This so-called phenomenon you described, it never really blocked women to move up the ladder. Or anyway I like to think it did not, not on my watch. – *Michael E., President and CEO, pharmaceutical industry.*

Yes, I've seen it happen once in a bad way. She was a colleague and I tried to help. Not during it, but afterwards you know. I tried to comfort her and be nice. During it I did not want to get involved. It was too complicated. It was bad! – *Conrad P., Executive VP and CFO, commercial real estate lender.*

I've seen it for sure. I've also seen women using men to take down other women for sure. Is that part of what you are referring to? That happens often! I think most guys are willing to go with it if the re-ward is worth it. I've done it – I helped my current boss get rid of a woman who was a threat to her and it got me a nice promotion and a fat bonus. It is all part of the game. – *Dave K., COO, tech industry.*

I'm a purist so I always try to get people to be up front and put their cards on the table. However, I've never really made a distinction between men and women in this regard, there can be rivalry and fighting in both instances. I guess I would say that women tend to help each other out more than men, no? If you find it not to be the case, maybe it's because it's taboo and I've missed it all! – *Howard B., Executive and GM, aerospace and transport industry.*

It is not taboo at all! Well let me correct this, it is taboo for women to admit it! We know better! – *J.C M., Executive Search Consultant.*

What you are describing here, this character of the conniving and mean woman using underhanded tactics to get her way and keep down other women … I mean, there has been one in every soap and drama since the beginning of television! I would not say it is taboo! Maybe it is taboo for women to admit to it. But then again, men are not exactly beating down doors to proclaim their deviousness either! Why would they? You know what I mean? – *Simon H., First Vice-President, investment financial institution.*

So, while a couple of the leaders we interviewed were prepared to take a stand, most seemed more comfortable shrugging it off from the sidelines. A minority of those we interviewed were prepared to use the conflict to their advantage to widen the chasm of gender inequality at the top. There were also those who said "it's a dog-eat-dog situation" and believed that everyone has to protect their own interests to survive in a tough, hyper-competitive working world.

Interestingly enough, we found men's reactions quite different when they had more skin in the game. To illustrate, we asked them how they would view women on women bullying if their daughters were on the receiving end of it. In those instances, our executives really put their boxing gloves on:

What you are describing amounts to intimidation and I don't and never stand for it, whoever or whatever the reason. Women can count on me to stand by them, I'm a rock. – *Kevin B., COO, automobile industry.*

What do I think about it? I think it does exist and that women should be more prepared for it. I mean, it does not serve anybody any good to be naive about it. I'm personally very sensitive to this issue. – *Sylvain T., Director of Human Resources, pharmaceutical industry.*

I don't tolerate it, never did and never will. It has never happened here but if it had, I would be all over it for sure. – *Sid R. National Sales Director, retail industry.*

To conclude our interviews, we asked our interviewees who had daughters of their own to offer some words of advice to anyone on the giving and receiving end of a bitch-fight incident. Their responses were stony serious. "I haven't raised my daughter to be a bully," was the most common response.

But what if their daughters were the target of a bullying female? Most of the fathers we spoke to said that they hoped their daughters would ask for help and fight back. Their ultimate take-home message was ominous. They said they would tell their daughters not to trust anyone at work and to watch their backs.

The Boys' Club

While not our intention, our asking about bullying also provoked many men to share with us their own stories about being intimidated or harassed at work.

Not surprisingly, their recollections were often very much like those recounted by the women we had met: tales of despair, fighting back and learning how to play the game better. However, one element in their story-telling really stood out – how important it was to be part of the *boys' club* to get ahead and be protected.

By definition, the *boys' club* refers to a group of peers, mostly informal, that exists in or out of the workplace and is used as a sounding board or a place to vent and seek advice.

Being part of this informal support group, which often means hanging out at bars after work or going to hockey and football games, was acknowledged as a critical stepping stone to accessing higher levels in their organisations. Forging these relationships and gaining sponsorship for future opportunities is the most powerful way to secure their position.

For our alphas, no matter how tough a work situation may become, being part of the boys' club ensured the head honchos at their organisations would have their best interests at heart and the path to greatness was on the horizon. They just had to take the occasional few shots on the chin and have faith.

Social research findings substantiate the important role that social support plays for those wanting to climb the corporate ladder. In particular, men seem more willing than women to engage in strategic networking to build these networks[26].

---

26 Kellerman, B., & Rhode, D. L. (Eds.). *Women and Leadership: The State of Play and Strategies for Change* (2007).

It is no surprise that many women demonstrate a general reluctance to network, and avoid social gatherings. Failing to engage at an informal level is a key reason why women more often than not lack the necessary relationships required to sponsor their candidacy for higher-order opportunities. This is not always the case. Social norms and traditional organisational cultures may also construct those concrete ceilings that women bang their heads on.

Case in point: a female client of ours worked at one of the big four corporations. She was on the partner track and shared how she was excluded from attending a director and partner cricket match because she was female. A new employee, a male director on the team poached from a competitor's organisation, was invited to participate. Our client has since lost her support to be considered for partner and the new recruit has been bumped into her place. There is no question that his ability to have access to the decision-makers in the partner fast-track process and her inability to form these important relationships blocked her career potential with the firm.

When push comes to shove, it is also a huge eye-opener to discover that women will usually select a male mentor or sponsor over a woman. This is because men are perceived by women as having more power and influence and women are seen as more of a threat to future career opportunities[27].

Eye of the Tiger

Men feel protected as members of the *boys' club*. However, similar girls' clubs appear few and far between. What group are women part of that makes them feel the same way? Most of the women we spoke to said it was more difficult for them to find support and community because they were always in competition with one another.

One of our interviewees, Stephanie, a business developer par excellence, described a star-studded women's group she had formed. Her idea was to gather together high potentials from different organisations to share best practices, exchange ideas and help each other out. She was successful in generating significant business from the contacts that she made in that group.

Stephanie's belief in getting these twelve high flyers together was that it was time for women to start supporting each other instead if being each others' stumbling blocks. Christine was very deliberate in the number of members she recruited for the group.

27   Hewlett, S.A, Peraino, K, Sherbin, L, and K. Sumberg, K. "The Sponsor Effect: Breaking Through the Last Glass Ceiling." *Harvard Business Review – Research Report* (2011), 1-85.

"More than twelve people and you lose control," she said. "We have enough barriers to job success. I really wanted to get a group of influential women together and see how we could change the world somehow."

The strategy of the group was to leverage the power in their positions to make decisions that would have real impact. It is true that the group became a powerful force of one voice in the Montreal job market. They carried a lot of clout and had made a collective decision to work together to get hired into senior roles in one particular company to take it over and lead it better.

Unfortunately, things didn't exactly go to plan.

"We couldn't believe it," Stephanie shared with us. "All this talk about supporting one another to make a difference was just bluster and hot air. From the beginning, we had all agreed that we were more powerful together then apart. We agreed to remove hierarchies and commit to a level playing field. And without question no men were allowed in the group under any circumstances. Then Marie-Claude shows up to our meeting with her arm around the current CEO. I was furious," she exclaimed. "When all was said and done the CEO did hire a few of us but we did not end up running the company or anything like that. Marie-Claude completely screwed that one up."

Stephanie could not get over the fact that Marie-Claude had double-crossed the group to feather her own nest. What made her particularly angry was the fact that a number of the group members were happy to accept second-rate positions that had been offered to them, rather than a shot at the big time that had been promised.

"Too many women are socialised to accept their lot in life," said Stephanie. "They are too comfortable playing second fiddle and accepting the scraps that are offered. It's sad really."

Listening to Stephanie's story, we couldn't help but think of a former psychoanalyst mentor of ours who encouraged his students to watch Desmond Morris's documentaries on the animal kingdom to understand human behaviour. Stephanie's story shed light on two distinct sets of human behaviours – those that bond us together for protection and for domination.

It is indeed a sobering realisation to acknowledge that the rules of the wild may actually apply to us human animals and extend to the concrete urban jungle that many of us now call home.

Advice for Daughters

During our research, we found a fair number of the leaders we interviewed wanted to know more about how to help their daughters prevent bullying attacks from other women. Upon reflection, some also wondered if they had not underplayed such occurrences before. They asked us for advice and while there is no magic formula, we gladly gave them a few take-aways to share and discuss with their loved ones.

Know Thyself

When it is all said and done, knowing thyself remains a simple but powerful piece of advice. Self-knowledge strengthens your immunity against bullies. Being acutely conscious of strengths and weaknesses bolsters your ammunition. Coupled with an unshakeable self-belief and an unwavering sense of self-worth you will be able to better cope with any onslaught thrown you way.

Become a Student of the Game

Remind people it is important to study the workplace environment and try to understand what the key stakeholders are all about. If one is in a highly competitive environment where prestige and power is at stake, it is better to be on guard. Observe what is going on. Ask questions. If you see someone being bullied and drawn into a bitch fight, don't be too happy about being off the hook. You may be next.

Figure out who is the female head honcho in the company. How did she get there? What are her drivers and motivations? Anybody you feel is overly cunning, sly or territorial?

Explore what's going at an organisational level. How do people play politics and get promoted? Who gets ahead? How do women get away with bitchy behaviours?

If somebody has difficulty responding to any of the above questions, they may not be sufficiently ready. Don't think the fact you don't take part in organisational politics shields you from not being drawn into it. Don't be naive. Be a student of the game and stay on the front foot.

Know the Signs

Are you getting some weird vibes from someone in your work group? Do you feel singled out? Do you suspect that someone might be undermining as she acts overly nice towards you? Don't take the matter lightly. There are all kinds of tools out there to help you get a better idea of the female psychopath/bully's modus operandi. Robert Hare's Psychopathy Checklist is one of the many examples that can be used for this exact purpose. It should of course be used with caution and the objective for the layman is not to form a differential diagnosis or master the scoring subtleties. The value is in the questions Hare offers to check for plausibility. Take notes and record what is going on; this will help you assess if a pattern is developing or if it's just a false alarm.

As a general rule, don't hesitate to read up on bullying – even if does not exactly cover your situation. There are multiple websites and books out there with all kinds of examples and references to help you get the skinny on this subject. In this day and age where information is at the tip of your fingers, there's no need to stay in the dark.

Shake it Off

Once you've noticed someone has put a target on your back, it's not always a bad idea to stay poised and avoid getting riled up after the first blows. We are not suggesting you let the bully step on you, but there is such a thing as overreacting. Bullies are attracted to those they can easily bring into their playing field. They are addicted to control, power and domination. The first blow is often a trap, a way for the bully to test the waters and see if the target will take the bait.

Don't take the bait. By responding with too much self-righteousness, you may be putting yourself at risk and exposing your vulnerability. Alternatively, ignoring and brushing it off can at times go a long way and those tactics, while not spectacular, should not be underestimated. You owe it to yourself to shrug it off at first and send the bully packing.

Build a Shield

Learning how to build a shield is a primary tactic to dealing with bullies. There's no such thing, of course, as impenetrable armour. Being a woman at work who is driven by an eagerness to please and be liked does not put you in good stead. Coupled with shaky self-confidence, this will make for a potentially bumpy road, especially if there are people surrounding you who test your resilience and ability to take one on the chin.

What's the solution? Make it your objective to boost your confidence over time. Take stock of what you bring to the table. Learn how to appreciate it and build on it. Don't be dependent on the approval of others but rather try to surround yourself with a selected entourage of people you can trust. Slowly learn how to manage those who disagree with you and bring yourself to live alongside a few who may be – God forbid – disappointed with either you or your work.

As one of our coaches told us recently, "The possibility of my boss being disappointed with my performance used to take up a staggering amount of my mental space! I was so consumed by it; I had forgotten that I was not exactly impressed with her management style either. This disappointment deal could work both ways! Remembering it helped me put things into perspective and muster up the courage to ask for better direction and clearer delegation. My performance improved overnight!"

Exit

Do you know somebody who is scared? Someone close is telling you that her boss is nuts; that she goes from loving people to hating people in a heartbeat. That manipulating others is second nature to her. You see there are some mean things going on, things that are not on the up and up. Things that can't be fix by a logical or calm explanation. Her boss is crazy. It's not that the environment is bringing out the worst in her. It's that she's using the environment to act out her mean streak.

In this case, it is worth considering that the solution may be to stay away from this person – psychopath or whatever else we may label her – as much as possible. Tell her it may be worth bringing it to HR higher ups or any other relevant authorities to make sure at least there's a record of what is going on. In Australia, if HR consider a staff member's health and safety to be at risk, they have an obligation to take action. There simply won't be a record. By all means, one can give it their best shot and see if someone out there is up for a fight. Or bite the bullet for a while; why not? But nobody should be miserable for too long. Trying to get relocated or leaving can be viable options. When things get too bad, there might not be much else to do. That's when you exit! It's a big world out there with many opportunities.

Mentors

And last but not least we pressed upon our male group to be there for their wives or daughters to act as a mentor. Don't underestimate what is going on. Be aware of the signs and offer a respectful ear. Take what they say seriously. Don't hesitate to nicely insist if they seem reluctant to share their feelings. Let them know you are by their side and that they can count on you.

Chapter 24 - Are You a Potential Target?

Anyone can find themselves on the receiving end of a bully's attack. The bitch knows no boundaries and is most often than not an equal-opportunity offender. Still, we have found there are things that women do wrong that make them most likely to be a target. It is important to point out those factors, because unlike so many things in the work life, knowing about them and doing something about it is actually within the realm of your control.

First up is the tendency to minimise people's mean streak and/or believe they are worth giving multiples chances. We have witnessed countless examples of successful leaders whose careers have come to an abrupt halt because of their belief that all people, even jerks who have proven themselves to be so, can change. Almost always, the leader is the one who ends up getting shoved out of the company and the renegade stays on, usually stepping into the leadership role pretty much unscathed. Why does it take some of us so long to take action with employees or colleagues who behave badly?

It's because most women prefer to believe in the good of people. Most of us want to give others the benefit of the doubt and believe in their ability to change. Most of us would also like to be thought of as kind and compassionate. But here's the truth. From a psychological perspective we know that after thirty years of age you're pretty much stuck with what you've got. A leopard isn't likely to change its spots. That is unless that leopard happens to go through some cataclysmic life event like a near-death experience, the loss of a loved one or the epiphany of finding God. We don't mean to sound cynical. We just know that to change behaviour at a fundamental level the electrical circuitry of the brain has to literally be jump started and re-wired for a person's behaviour to truly change.

As a leader, not taking swift action and removing people who behave badly can result in disrespect from others and, potentially, the end of your own career with that organisation as you know it.

At the first sniff of deceit, we advised Kathryn to report the conflict of interest between Emma and Preston and cancel her involvement in the recruitment process. Kathryn felt this would be premature and wanted to wait to give Emma a go in spite of her better judgment. In the end, Kathryn cut off all contact with Emma, but only after a full month of Emma undermining her by spreading rumours about her incompetence and talking up Preston's alleged superiority for the role. The damage to Kathryn's reputation was difficult to quantify, but we knew for sure that her candidacy had been significantly and irreparably tainted. The playing field was not even and Preston had the upper hand right from the get-go. In the end Kathryn did strong-arm Emma into turning herself in, but it was too little too late. She had not moved fast enough. A tough lesson to learn.

The golden rule here is if you know a colleague, staff member or client is doing things to undermine you, we recommend acting swiftly to remove them before the situation bites you in the butt. Trust your instincts, aim and fire!

Playing Politics is Only for Arse-holes

We met an outstanding amount of women who simply refused to engage in any political games whatsoever. They felt it was dirty and did not want to embark on that slippery slope. Or they did not feel they were good at it so they did not see the point. Others played the ethical card and claimed this was beneath them.

Obviously everybody makes their own choice and has their own limits as to what they can and can't do in the name of politics. As long as you are aware of the consequences that staying on the sidelines means, that's quite fine.

As a general rule, we find women should do more at a political level as there is a way to play politics and stay true to your values.

The number-one priority is to build relationships. The key here is to start with the people you like and with whom connecting requires minimal efforts. In coaching terms when discussing the quality of key strategic relationships, we refer to the level of energy required into building or maintaining the connection as the level of nurture. This term is not new and is commonly used amongst sales professionals. We ask our clients, "What is the level of nurture required in this relationship? Is it low, medium or high?" The response dictates the amount of energy required to improve or maintain the relationship.

In our main story, we found that Kathryn chose to spend too much time with her head down, making sure she was focused on the daily grind, meeting deadlines and producing great quality work. This is such a common mistake it's not funny. She would have been much better served to spend more time on understanding the motivations and behaviours of others and thus enhance the quality of her relationships with significant players.

Being better connected would have paved the way for a much fairer fight.

Finding Your Authentic Voice

Another challenge is to find the right way to be confident and assertive. Many women struggle with that one. Too often they go from a quiet and understanding stance to being overly pushy and hell-bent on telling it like it is. There is no sufficient middle ground or, to put it in different terms, it takes them a while to find their right voice.

Being able to find an authentic voice that commands respect and inspires confidence is key point to keep bullies at bay. For Kathryn this was especially challenging. For years she had a tendency to dilute the power of her communication by using phrases like "I'm sorry," "Could you do me a favour," and "I was wondering if there was any way you could ...." The first really visible step in Kathryn's shift required her to be conscious of it and actively change the way she spoke to get things done. This meant resisting padding her dialogue and learning to become more direct and straightforward.

Kathryn tried, but like so many other women, her shift from doormat to warrior was quite dramatic. Fuelled partly by her ambitions and partly by the repressed anger she had been feeling over the years as a result of putting her own needs on the back burner, she went all out.

She suddenly told the truth! As coaches our job is to speak the truth and help others find theirs. This however does not mean a leader should always say what they are really thinking no matter what.

The fact of the matter is that too much truth can lead to your demise and fast. It is our belief that deep down, most people can't handle it. They don't want to hear bad news and are unprepared to deal with the brutal facts, or to look in the mirror – particularly if that truth is about them.

As Charles de Gaulle once said, "Every leader must stage manage their effects." Successful leadership requires the leader to be an organisational politician skilled in the art of transforming into a chameleon and changing skin when required. We're not suggesting that leaders be liars. But what we are suggesting is careful planning around how to present a view that may be taboo or contrary to popular perception. It needs to be done skilfully and gracefully to be digestible.

At some point in her journey, Kathryn got fed up and decided to hit them all between the eyes and raised all the contentious truths she could muster. We respected Kathryn's grape-fruit-sized balls attitude, but feared that behind the clapping and smiles it provoked more shock than admiration. In hindsight, her change was too drastic and thus ill-advised.

To her credit, she was smart enough to recognise it and in time, made significant improvements. Developing her own memorable and unique voice was a key factor in preparing herself for high-level politics.

You should do the same; there is no reason not to.

Impression Management

It's a proven fact we have about seven seconds to make a good impression. If we had a dollar for how many times we've spoken to our coaching clients about being well groomed, making the most of all their physical assets, having good manners, and dressing to impress to be more successful, we'd own our own paradise island by now. Wearing a fabulous smile is also priceless.

What's interesting is the reaction we get. More often than not our clients look at us like we are either full of it, or deeply superficial. The bottom line is this is serious business – so much so that professionals like Diane Craig, a very well-networked image and etiquette consultant from Ottawa in Canada, makes a great living from helping politicians and international dignitaries overhaul their image to get more votes and increase their likeability quotient (or LQ). Yes, there's even a profession that provides a service like this. Likeability quotient is defined as the "level of happiness and well being that you arise in others[28]." In the same way the reverse is true. The more unpleasant others find you, the more difficulties you are likely to encounter in life and at work. Honest.

So, as much of a cad as Preston Steele was, he knew the benefits of having a well-managed image and did what he had to do to maintain a high LQ. He was naturally a happy and passionate guy. People left conversations with him feeling motivated, energized and on a high. His smile alone left others bedazzled. Kathryn was equally passionate, but far more serious in nature. People respected Kathryn's intellect; however, they did not usually invite her out for drinks.

Preston made himself well-liked by noticing the details about people and really listening. You've heard the expression, "it's the little things that make a difference." Preston, like so many others, had this down pat. He remembered people's birthdays, the names of their spouses and partners, and had a great memory for recalling people's hobbies and interests. This meant most people felt valued after talking to Preston, as if he had really listened because he remembered the minutia about their lives. On one of the few occasions he interacted with us, he showed us this technique he used to remember

28   Olivola, C. Y., & Todorov, A. "Elected in 100 Milliseconds: Appearance-based Trait Inferences and Voting." *Journal of Nonverbal Behavior* (2010), 34(2), 83-110.

things. When he made a new contact he'd write down a few things about them he'd learned on the back on their business card. That way if he ever had to connect with them again he had something to talk about. It was a great conversation starter, and people were always super-impressed he'd remembered some small detail about them. We'd heard a rumour from others who knew him well that he used to boast about his technique being a leg opener. Pretty crass, but you've still got to hand it to him. It was a clever strategy on all fronts.

Preston's rugged good looks didn't hurt him either. Sex sells and Preston used his physical assets to full advantage. He looked like he could already be a Chief Executive Officer with his well-styled locks and perfectly pressed suits. Research into upping your LQ shows an exponential rise when attractiveness is added to the mix. Kathryn was an equally stunning woman; however, she tended not to dress up enough so her good looks were not a focus. She wanted to be taken seriously. We're not sure whether this helped or hindered her. Being a good-looking woman does not always work to your advantage with other women, but it wouldn't have hurt her popularity with the male contingent, that's for sure.

At the end of the day, despite Preston's unscrupulous tactics for getting in the door at Kudos, there remains nonetheless a lot to be learned about getting ahead from the powerful tactics he utilized to leverage himself at Kudos and become a formidable contender for the top job.

We dare ask: are you making the most of what you have to offer?

Chapter 25 – Make Love, Not War

The truth is out. It is not exclusively men strengthening the glass ceiling and pushing women over the glass cliff. The way some women treat each other at work is a very real barrier to women getting ahead. By opposing any attempts of other females to advance in their careers, women are perpetuating the cultural stigmas already held against women in the workplace.

If we listen to the researchers, we may argue that women have no control over being nasty, that women can not make conscious choices. We discriminate unconsciously. Unconscious discrimination is defined as the act of unknowingly discriminating against someone. Whether you choose to believe it or not, we all do it consciously or not. Our biases affect not only our world-view but also influence our decision-making, sometimes without us even knowing.

It would be unrealistic to suggest that we can eliminate unconscious biases forever. However, being more aware of this tendency may enable people to limit its impact on how we behave, and create more mindful decision-making. Becoming more well-informed about how we are responding to our workplace cultures can only increase our conscious awareness, so that deciding whether to be nasty or not becomes a conscious choice.

You are not entitled to bully someone because you've been bullied before. Just because you feel that's the way it goes in your organisation, doesn't make it right. You can't justify being a bully by saying you can't help it, or justify it by calling it tough love. Think twice. Acknowledge your inner mean streak and fight off your more or less conscious drive to be a jerk. There is surely another way. You owe it to everybody to find it and improve.

One only has to return to our chimps to find substantiation for this. There exists a breed of pygmy chimpanzees called bonobos. Their chimp society has a dominant matriarchal culture where females are higher in social standing than males and govern the tribe. Describing them as "peace-loving primates[29]," primatologist Frans de Waal states bonobos are indeed capable of altruism, compassion, empathy, kindness, patience, and sensitivity. He describes bonobo society as a "gynaecocracy" meaning "women's government over women and men" or "women's social supremacy." Interestingly, researchers of bonobos have found minimal aggression takes place between the sexes and that conflict is usually resolved by "making love and not war."

---

29   Frans de Waal. *Peacemaking among Primates.* Cambridge: Harvard Business Review Press, 1989.

What is clear to us is that the key to creating a uniform playing field rests in the hands of all women. Women must be more aware of their biological drives, their unconscious biases and behaviours that inadvertently block and punish members of the sisterhood at work.

Seeking to work together is the way to increase female representation at the top, thereby decreasing the need to play dirty politics to get ahead. It is obvious that a woman-against-woman career strategy will not get us any closer. Not supporting each other is one of the greatest threats to all of us having the life we want.

Upon reflection on the bonobos, you cannot help but wonder how different things would be if women ruled the world. A romantic and unlikely scenario, we know. Perhaps the more pertinent questions we really need to be asking are what would happen if women around the world supported each other? What could be achieved if women of the world were united and focussed on working together to build a community of equals? Could it then be all about love? Or how about all about love and better sex? That's much more of a promising scenario!

ABOUT THE AUTHORS

Vanessa Vershaw, M.Psych (Org) MAPS

Vanessa Vershaw is an Australian organisational psychologist, coach and former journalist with extensive international consulting experience. As an executive level practitioner, Vanessa is a highly regarded, trusted advisor to c-suite leaders and Fortune 500 organisations. She has successfully managed both leadership and large-scale organisational development initiatives with executive teams and companies around the globe.

An engaging business leader, Vanessa is passionate about developing leadership capabilities and unlocking and harnessing their potential. She is known for her ability to assist her clients through deep and sustainable transformation and life-changing impact. She is also recognized as an engaging presenter and with great storyteller ability. Vanessa is frequently invited to give seminars and speeches as a subject matter expert in all areas of people and organizational performance.

Vanessa is the managing director at Reinvention Organisation & Leadership Consulting and has an undergraduate degree in foreign languages and the dramatic arts. She has a postgraduate diploma in journalism, a bachelor of psychology, and a master's degree in organisational psychology. She is also a national media spokesperson for the Australian College of Organisational Psychology.

Vanessa is fluent in English, French and Italian and lives in Perth, Australia with her husband Jason and their two children, Noah and Allegra.

More information at reinventionconsulting.com.au.

Jean-François Ducharme, Ph.D.

Dr. Ducharme is a Canadian organisational psychologist, author and coach. Jean-François helps people improve their efficiency at work, develop their potential and overcome interpersonal conflicts. An assessment specialist and passionate writer, he has interviewed hundreds of leaders in order to better understand how they perceive success, are driven to reach the top, and manage their work environment. A respected coach, he has guided many leaders to better position themselves and triumph within an ever-demanding business world.

Very interested by all things storytelling, he founded a company – D.W. Creation, Ties, Lies and Leadership – that is about developing and promoting entertaining leadership/managing content. He is presently putting the finishing touch on his first novel, a funny story about coaching, finding his true voice and leveraging one's gimmick to the max.

He holds a Ph.D. in psychology from the Université du Québec à Montréal. He started his career working with street kids, a group of people from whom he learned a lot. A dedicated family man, he lives in Montreal with his long-time fiancée and kids.

Jean-François can be reached at jefducharme@hotmail.com.

Also by Jean-Francois Ducharme:

Gagner sa vie sans la perdre. La fonction de l'argent au travail et dans ses choix de carrière. Québec Livres (2013).

Gérer la pression au travail. Des repères pour le gestionnaire ambitieux. Éditions Quebecor (2011).

Mieux diriger sans se fatiguer. Éditions Quebecor (2009).

Contact us:

Website: http://www.bitchfight.com.au/

Facebook: https://www.facebook.com/
Bitch-Fight-175714859441396

Instagram: https://www.instagram.com/bitchfightbook/

Twitter: https://twitter.com/bitchfight_book

www.ingramcontent.com/pod-product-compliance
Lightning Source LLC
Chambersburg PA
CBHW071520200326
41519CB00019B/6020